OSPREY COMBAT AIRCRAFT • 55

USAF F-4 PHANTOM II MiG KILLERS 1972–73

SERIES EDITOR: TONY HOLMES

OSPREY COMBAT AIRCRAFT • 55

USAF F-4 PHANTOM II MiG KILLERS 1972–73

PETER E DAVIES

OSPREY
PUBLISHING

First published in Great Britain in 2005 by Osprey Publishing,
Midland House, West Way, Botley, Oxford OX2 0PH, UK
44-02 23rd St, Suite 219, Long Island City, NY 11101, USA
E-mail: info@ospreypublishing.com

Transferred to digital print on demand 2010

First published 2005
2nd impression 2008

Printed and bound by PrintOnDemand-Worldwide.com, Peterborough, UK

A CIP catalogue record for this book is available from the British Library

ISBN: 978 1 84176 657 7

Edited by Tony Holmes
Page design by Tony Truscott
Cover Artwork by Mark Postlethwaite
Aircraft Profiles by Jim Laurier
Scale Drawings by Mark Styling
Index by Alan Thatcher
Originated by PPS Grasmere Ltd, Leeds, UK
Typeset in Adobe Garamond, Rockwell and Univers

Acknowledgements

The author and editor are very grateful to the following F-4 MiG killers for their assistance
with this project;Lt Col James R Bell, USAF (Ret), Brig Gen Dan Cherry, USAF (Ret),
Col Gordon Clouser, USAF (Ret), Col James Cooney, USAF (Ret), Col Chuck DeBellevue,
USAF (Ret), Lt Col Wayne Frye, USAF (Ret), Col Philip W Handley, USAF (Ret), Capt
Doug Hardgrave, USAF (Ret), Col James Hendrickson, USAF (Ret), Capt Leigh Hodgdon,
USAF (Ret), Maj Paul Howman, USAF (Ret), Capt Robert H Jasperson, USAF (Ret),
Lt Col Keith W Jones Jr, USAF (Ret), Col Joe Kittinger, USAF (Ret), Lt Col Bruce Leonard,
USAF, (Ret), Lt Col Stuart Maas, USAF (Ret), Col John Madden, USAF (Ret), Capt Michael
J Mahaffey, USAF (Ret), Lt Col Douglas Malloy, USAF (Ret), Lt Col John D Markle, USAF
(Ret), Col Ivy McCoy, USAF (Ret), Lt Col Harry McKee, USAF (Ret), Capt Fred Olmsted
USAF (Ret), Maj Lawrence H Pettit, USAF (Ret), Lt Col Stan Pickett, USAF (Ret), Lt Col
Fred Sheffler, USAF (Ret) and Capt Michael D Vahue, USAF (Ret). Sincere thanks are also
owed to Tom Brewer, Col Michael P Cooper, USAF (Ret), Kim Dietel, Michael France,
Chris Hobson, Alan Howarth, Col Bill F McDonald, USAF (Ret), Leroy Pfaff, John Poole,
Peter Schinkelshoek and Norm Taylor. Finally, particular thanks are due to
Col Ron Thurlow, USAF (Ret) for his unstinting support and encouragement.

Front cover

15 October 1972 saw one of the fiercest MiG
encounters of the Operation Linebacker period,
resulting in the destruction of three MiG-21s.
'Chevy' flight was the third MiGCAP formation for
a large, Ubon-based F-4 strike in the Hanoi area.
It was led by Maj Ivy McCoy and his Weapon
Systems Operator (WSO), Maj Fred Brown, in
F-4D 66-7463. This famous aircraft had been
assigned to Capts Steve Ritchie and Chuck
DeBellevue for Ritchie's fifth kill at the end of
August, and it probably still bore the worn,
white-stencilled names of its former 'owners'
on its nose.

'Chevy' flight moved in to meet a wave of
MiGs as the previous MiGCAP ('Buick' flight)
headed for the tankers. Ivy McCoy initially
passed the MiGs head-on in cloud. Turning
quickly through 180 degrees at an altitude of
12,000 ft, he saw contrails at his 'one o'clock'
position and then observed MiGs descending
ahead and slightly to the right of his flight path.
He turned behind them as Fred Brown
unsuccessfully attempted to get a radar lock and
released three AIM-7E-2s in quick succession.
All three missiles fell away without guiding.

Maj McCoy followed the MiG in a shallow,
20-degree banking turn and fired three AIM-9E
Sidewinders. The third missile detonated just
250 ft ahead of the F-4D, and very close to the
MiG's tailpipe. The rear fuselage of the North
Vietnamese jet began to burn and disintegrate,
causing its pilot to eject. Ivy McCoy noted that
the time was 1425.40 hrs exactly.

After 66-7463's fourth MiG kill on 10 May 1972,
Steve Ritchie and the jet's crew chief, Sgt
Reginald Taylor, had intended to name the F-4D
'Smash Four'. Although this nickname was never
painted on the jet, it acquired a sixth kill marking
after McCoy and Brown's victory, making it the
highest-scoring US combat aircraft since the
Korean War.

Soon after its 15 October success, the
Phantom II's left splitter plate was repainted to
show all six victory stars, and these were carried
in various configurations right up until the fighter
was put on permanent display at the Air Force
Academy in Colorado Springs in May 1987.

(*Cover artwork by Mark Postlethwaite.*)

FOR A CATALOGUE OF ALL BOOKS PUBLISHED BY OSPREY
MILITARY AND AVIATION PLEASE CONTACT:

Osprey Direct, c/o Random House Distribution Center,
400 Hahn Road, Westminster, MD 21157
Email: uscustomerservice@ospreypublishing.com

Osprey Direct, The Book Service Ltd, Distribution Centre,
Colchester Road, Frating Green, Colchester, Essex, CO7 7DW
E-mail: customerservice@ospreypublishing.com

www.ospreypublishing.com

CONTENTS

CHAPTER ONE
ECHOES OF *ROLLING THUNDER* 6

CHAPTER TWO
SKIRMISHES 12

CHAPTER THREE
***LINEBACKER* LAUNCHED 25**

CHAPTER FOUR
ACE MAKING 43

CHAPTER FIVE
BACKING THE 'BUFFS' 66

APPENDICES 86
COLOUR PLATES COMMENTARY 90
INDEX 96

ECHOES OF *ROLLING THUNDER*

Rapid development of the basic F-4B Phantom II from 1962-65 resulted in the F-4C, reconnaissance RF-4B/C and F-4D/J. With the F-4E, the US Air Force showed that it had effectively taken over the Phantom II programme, and it went on to buy three times as many F-4s as the US Navy. By 1967 F-4s equipped two-thirds of the USAF's tactical fighter wings, and the gun-armed F-4E – the most radical re-design of the basic F-4 – was introduced in October of that year.

Bruce Leonard, who completed his first combat tour as an F-4 'Guy In Back' ('GIB') at Da Nang, converted to the front seat and returned in 1972 for a second tour that included a MiG kill. He felt that the 'F-4E rear cockpit gave the back-seater something to work with, unlike earlier F-4s, even though it took away his forward visibility. In the F-4C the radar was mainly for looking at targets against clear sky or boats on the water. However, the F-4 was a lovely aeroplane, being proven and reliable'. Its main problem, as with all Phantom IIs, was summed up by the former 555th TFS Ops Officer, Col Mike Cooper. 'It was such a fuel hog. Fuel consumption was always foremost in your mind'.

F-4Ds, introduced towards the end of Operation *Rolling Thunder*, enjoyed great success throughout the renewed fighting in 1971-73. Indeed, they destroyed 27 MiGs, compared with 23 for the F-4E. In MiG killer Lt Col John Markle's estimation, 'the D-model was a good flying machine with a number of eccentricities that had to be lived with. The stick was "heavy" at different parts of the performance envelope, and had to be trimmed throughout. The cockpit wasn't crowded – switches were reasonably arranged by mission, but their accessibility wasn't ideal. Several of the weapons switches were on the pedestal below the front instrument panel and in front of the stick. I recall the interior lighting was not good for night sorties. We used masking tape to reduce the intensity

The 390th TFS 'Wild Boars' was one of the longest-serving units in Vietnam. It was first assigned to the 366th TFW 'Gunfighters' at Da Nang AB in October 1966, remaining there until deactivation in June 1972. Despite its long exposure to combat, the squadron claimed just one MiG kill (on 1 May 1967), and even that was achieved through 'manoeuvring' a MiG-17 into the ground, rather than with a missile. The F-4D's radar was preferred to the F-4E's for air-to-air missions because its larger scanner dish gave slightly longer detection ranges (*Norm Taylor*)

and minimise the glare on the canopy at night – this was unnecessary in the better-lit F-4E. Lack of air-conditioning in that climate was a problem, but the biggest disadvantages were the limited rearward visibility from either seat, and the fact that the engines smoked, except in 'burner'.

It was also a tough aircraft. Triple MiG killer John Madden put 10g on an F-4 while evading a SAM in 1972. The massive force broke the front mounts on both J79 engines, dropping then down within the fuselage, but they continued to run well enough to get him home.

GUNSHIP F-4s

Rolling Thunder experience in the challenging conditions over North Vietnam had shown that missiles were an uncertain means of scoring a kill in many circumstances. Visual identification (VID) of a target was usually needed, partly due to unreliable Identification Friend or Foe (IFF) equipment that exposed USAF aircraft to the risk of 'blue on blue' losses. This denied the AIM-7 principal advantage of beyond visual range (BVR) operation. Often, pilots launched AIM-7s too close to their targets for their guidance and fusing systems to work properly. During the entire war, 612 AIM-7s were fired by Phantom IIs for a total of just 56 confirmed kills. For the AIM-9 the figures were slightly better, with 454 launches resulting in 81 kills – an 18 per cent success rate.

Many F-4 pilots felt that they missed kill opportunities during close-in fighting because they had no gun. McDonnell Douglas had worked on cannon-armed F-4 ideas since 1961, but an internal gun was omitted until Vietnam. With the F-4D, the USAF got better bombing capability and a lead-computing sight (both lacking in the F-4C). In October 1963 Tactical Air Command (TAC) requested a new, gun-armed jet with many other improvements. This evolved into the F-4E, planned around the Hughes CORDS (Coherent On-Receive Doppler System) radar.

Lt Leigh Hodgdon (left, seen here with Maj John Kikta) was WSO for the second MiG kill of 1972, with Lt Col J W Kittinger as aircraft commander. Joe Kittinger was already a legendary figure in the USAF, which he joined in 1949. As a test pilot, he had made two record-breaking balloon descents in a full-pressure suit from 102,800 ft to test astronaut escape gear, reaching 614 mph in free-fall. He flew three combat tours, totalling 485 missions. The first of these was with the 1st Air Commando *Farm Gate*, flying B-26B Invaders (*L Hodgdon*)

F-4E-35-MC 67-0301 was one of the earliest F-4Es in South-east Asia, but one of the last to kill a MiG in 1972. Seen here in 1969, it bears an assortment of bombs and Bullpup missiles (*Peter Schinkelshoek*)

CORDS proved too complex, causing delays in the programme until it was dropped in January 1968. Instead, the Westinghouse AN/APQ-120 radar/fire control system was used when it became available in December 1967 – 30 F-4Es had already been delivered by then. Solid-state electronics and a smaller, elliptical radar antenna enabled the system, with its AN/APQ-109 radar, to fit into the new, pointed nose.

Further additions were an F-4J-type slotted stabiliser ('a real benefit to manoeuvrability' according to veteran Bruce Leonard), up-rated J79-GE-17 engines and a new 104-gallon fuel tank in the upper rear fuselage to counterbalance the enlarged nose. The USAF ordered 993 F-4Es for its own use, making it the most numerous Phantom II variant.

LESSONS PARTLY LEARNED

In the four years between *Rolling Thunder* and the resumption of air combat over North Vietnam, there were many opportunities to apply the experience of the first five years of war. The F-4E was one outcome, although the impact of its gun armament on the next phase of the conflict was not decisive – it played a major part in only seven of the F-4E's 23 kills. Other innovations, particularly the introduction of APX-80 *Combat Tree* IFF interrogation devices, were equally important. This equipment enabled F-4D crews to identify MiGs at considerable range and use their AIM-7 missiles in BVR mode.

There was also considerable debate after *Rolling Thunder* concerning fighter tactics, focused on the Weapons Systems and Evaluation Group's *Red Baron I* study. This analysed the *Rolling Thunder* fights in exhaustive detail, and a principal conclusion was that awareness of the exact location of the enemy aircraft, so that a position of advantage could be attained, was the single most significant factor in an aerial victory. In over 80 per cent of US MiG kills, American pilots began the duel from a position of advantage, and that figure was higher (87 per cent) in the case of MiG pilots who downed US jets. Almost half the MiG pilots who were shot down probably never saw their attackers, while nearly 60 per cent of US casualties were lost in that situation. MiG pilots, with excellent ground control, and fighting close to home in small fighters that were hard to see, could often be vectored into positions from which they could gain a firing position from behind or below, undetected by the Americans.

Often, F-4 attack formations were made more vulnerable because they had to fly a rigid 'pod formation' to maximise protection from their ECM pods. The USAF's tight 'fluid four' standard formations, with two elements (pairs) of fighters, meant two wingmen having to concentrate on protecting their leaders, and keeping close formation with them, thereby increasing their vulnerability and reducing their chances of a shot at a MiG – even if they were allowed one by the designated 'shooter' (the flight or element leader). Conversely, leaders had to avoid losing their wingmen during a manoeuvring fight, particularly if they were inexperienced. Stu Maas, a MiG killer in April 1972, recalled;

'We had pilots that came straight out of the replacement training units (RTU) at George, Davis-Monthan and McDill AFBs. They had only a basic capability to fly good air combat. Perhaps that's why we flew the wingmen in such rigid formations (besides the need for 'pod' formations), "lead to the weakest link". Our flight leads were, for the

Paveway laser-guided bombs occupy the pylons on F-4D-24-MC 66-0274 of the 435th TFS/8th TFW at Ubon in 1972. This aircraft was a 555th TFS MiG killer for Capt Don Logeman and 1Lt Fred McCoy in October 1967. Reassigned to the 435th TFS (via the 12th and 366th TFWs), it survived the war. By 1972 Udorn F-4s had taken over most of the MiGCAP duties, leaving the former MiG-slaying 8th TFW 'Wolfpack' units to concentrate on bombing (*via Peter Schinkelshoek*)

most part, senior captains and majors with more experience, but the air-to-air area was pretty new to all but the Nellis Fighter Weapons School folks and the few RTU instructors who taught ACM to the new F-4 crews. At that time, there were no uniquely tasked air-to-air F-4 wings to draw talent from. In 1969-73 the F-4 RTUs were grinding out crews every few weeks, and most were headed to South-east Asia.'

Several four-ship MiGCAP flights were usually needed to cover an attack so that they could deal with threats from different directions. CAPs covered the ingress and egress of each flight, while a third would orbit to protect the attack flights over the target area. MiG pilots quickly learned to draw MiGCAP flights or elements away from the strike flights, using one or two MiGs to do so, while a third slipped in to attack the strikers.

The US Navy's 'loose deuce' tactics, using two widely spaced F-4s giving mutual support and equal right to fire on an available target, had proved successful, and some USAF officers tried to introduce it as a better means of utilising escort fighter assets. However, established 'fighting wing' USAF tactics generally prevailed throughout the war. Partly, this was because air-to-air combat, and the training required for it, took a low priority in an Air Force that had bombing as the primary mission for its Phantom IIs. Indeed, air-to-air training was actively discouraged by many senior officers as being dangerous and unnecessary.

Red Baron also highlighted the comparatively poor performance and reliability of the AIM-4, AIM-7 and AIM-9, attributing many failures to the pilots' tendency to fire them inside minimum range, or in turning fights that exceeded the missiles' tracking capability. Although the F-4E brought improvements (the more ergonomic '556 Mod' radar/cockpit refit in late 1972), it still relied on the same missiles as previous variants.

Rather than replace the original AIM-9B with a version of the USN-sponsored AIM-9D the USAF procured the AIM-9E. This was essentially an AIM-9B with a sharper, more aerodynamic nose and a Peltier thermo-electric cooler to give the seeker head slightly more sensitivity to heat sources. The AIM-9E could be fired at a greater angle of aspect off its target, as well as at greater range. It remained the principal AIM-9 variant throughout 1972-73, but scored only six kills from F-4s.

Meanwhile, the USAF developed its own Philco-Ford AIM-9J variant. Tests in ideal conditions produced good results, but they had to be matched in the field, and combat testing began on 8 June 1972 with the 432nd TRW at Udorn RTAFB. The first AIM-9J combat sortie was flown on 2 August by the 555th and 13th TFSs, but no firings were made that month (apart from one inadvertent release). Its first use against MiGs was on 9 September 1972 when 'Olds' flight was jumped by two MiG-19s as they left the target. 'Olds' 3 (Capts John Madden and Chuck DeBellevue) fired three AIM-9Js and destroyed both MiGs with them, giving DeBellevue ace status with six kills in all. The AIM-9J's reputation was further enhanced when it became clear that their second missile, which did not score, was actually launched in error.

However, in a similar encounter on 16 September, four 'Chevy' flight 'Triple Nickel' F-4Es pursued a lone MiG-21 at low altitude, fired four AIM-9Js and not one of them hit the target. Another four were then launched by 'Chevy 3', and the last of these destroyed the MiG. The chase had been straight and level, with little manoeuvring. Clearly, the other seven missiles had all failed at low altitude. This incident revealed that the AIM-9J's effective range was less than predicted.

The final, AIM-9J kill came on 15 October 1972 when a *Combat Tree* F-4D flown by Majs Ivy McCoy and Fred Brown fired three AIM-7s at a MiG-21, followed by three AIM-9Js. The final Sidewinder was the only missile to find its target. Out of 31 attempted AIM-9J launches in 1972-73, only four scored kills – 23 missed and four remained on the rail.

SUPER SPARROW?

In fact, the low 'scores' for the Sidewinder – the preferred missile for *Rolling Thunder* – coincided with a preference for the AIM-7 Sparrow during *Linebacker II*. It too suffered reliability problems. From 2 September until 29 December 1972, 100 of the improved AIM-7E-2 'Dogfight' Sparrows were fired, resulting in only five kills. In the same period, 24 AIM-9Es were released for only two confirmed kills. However, 30 of the 50 F-4 aerial kills between 21 February 1972 and the end of hostilities did result from AIM-7E-2 launches. These variable results echoed the experience of several *Rolling Thunder* battles.

AIM-4Ds were also employed, but their lack of a proximity fuse was a major handicap. Most missed their targets by less than 20 ft, without exploding. According to Col Bill McDonald, the AIM-4D was also 'much too sensitive to any jarring, or even stray voltage misalignment'. Most of the F-4Ds operated by the 555th TFS in 1971-72 were still wired for the AIM-4D, despite its lack of success in *Rolling Thunder*. Col Mike Cooper of the 555th TFS recalled, 'We did everything in our power to get them abolished. They were useless. A friend told me I was due for a ticket

A massive load of cluster bomb units and Mk 82 bombs leaves no space for defensive missiles on this 34th TFS/388th TFW F-4E. In January 1971, when this photograph was taken, the chances of a MiG encounter were slight in any case (*Don Jay*)

With its bomb racks now empty, a 'Gunfighters' (390th TFS/366th TFW) F-4D-31-MC returns to Da Nang AB on 17 April 1971. This particular Phantom II (66-7678) had been flown by Col Chuck Yeager when it was assigned to the 4th TFW in 1967-69. The F-4's massive centreline fuel tank had to be jettisoned carefully prior to air-to-air combat, as it could easily damage the aircraft's belly, aft Sparrow missiles or stabilator as it parted company with the Phantom II (*Norm Taylor*)

from the Environmental Protection people for littering the countryside with damned little AIM-4s! I fired off more than a dozen. It was ineffective, and twice the price of an AIM-9'.

In retrospect, he wished his unit had been more proactive in trying to convert more F-4Ds to AIM-9s, as Col Robin Olds had tried to do in 1967, but they were always being told that the missile was, 'good, and about to start working properly any day now. Even flying through a light rain shower at 400 knots would craze the transparency on the seeker head so that it wouldn't work. These were not replaced. Maintenance on them was virtually non-existent'.

'Dogfight' Sparrow was a response to poor results with AIM-7s during *Rolling Thunder*, when 260 firings yielded only 20 confirmed USAF kills. Many had been launched at low altitudes, inside minimum range parameters or salvoed against manoeuvring targets. None of these situations gave the missile a realistic chance. AIM-7E-2 was designed to operate at shorter range and higher g. It could be adapted to 'dogfight' mode by installing an electronic 'minimum range' plug in its side, allowing the missile to guide from a launch at a range of 1500 ft (rather than 3300 ft for the standard AIM-7E) against a non-manoeuvring target flying at the same speed as the F-4. It also tracked manoeuvring targets better than its predecessors, held 'radar lock' better and had improved fusing. When the war went 'hot' again in 1972, US fighters fired 243 Sparrows, many of them AIM-7E-2s.

Results were still disappointing because of the conditions in which they were used – 65 per cent missed their targets, often because they were fired outside operational parameters. Some were ripple-fired to distract enemy pilots and force them to fly into the path of a follow-up shot, or to divert MiGs from attacks on strike F-4s. But there were still numerous technical problems with motor ignition, guidance and fusing. Added to this were maintenance difficulties. Missiles were trucked over rough roads to test facilities for calibration, with consequent vibration damage. Often, they were repeatedly uploaded and downloaded from jets as ordnance configurations changed between 'bombing' and 'air-to-air' missions.

Despite these problems, the experience of *Linebacker* showed that when the missiles worked, they were far superior to any air-to-air weapon that the enemy could field.

SKIRMISHES

President Richard Nixon's 'bombing pause' from 1 November 1968 enabled North Vietnam to rebuild and improve battered airfields and to extend its air defence network into Laotian airspace. Many new MiG pilots were also trained. In 1965 the Vietnamese Peoples' Air Force (VPAF) had 36 MiG pilots and aircraft, and this figure had risen to 72 pilots and 180 aircraft by 1968. In May 1970 there were 140 MiG-17s, 95 MiG-21s and 30 MiG-19s on strength. By January 1972, the 921st Fighter Regiment (FR) had converted onto the improved MiG-21MF, which had a longer range, better interception radar and could carry four (rather than two) R-3S/R 'Atoll' air-to-air missiles. Some pilots also began to qualify in night flying.

Throughout 1969-70, the progressive reduction in American forces in South-east Asia removed the *Rivet Top/College Eye* EC-121s from their mission-controlling orbits. The remaining tactical jets concentrated on interdiction of the Ho Chi Minh trails, and MiGs only occasionally threatened these missions from new bases closer to the demilitarised zone (DMZ). VPAF efforts centred on downing B-52s on *Arc Light* sorties in order to reap the immense propaganda coup such a victory would bring with it. Although no 'Buffs' were actually lost, MiG pilots came close on several occasions. Their near success forced TAC to establish F-4 'hot pad' alerts at Udorn and Da Nang, although as 555th TFS operations officer Mike Cooper pointed out, the Phantom II crews actually had very little to do. 'The number of active scrambles that achieved anything was negligible. It was almost a waste of time and resources'.

Fearing an eventual invasion of South Vietnam, the Pentagon once again contemplated bombing the threatening build-up of military supplies in the North. However, the Nixon administration chose instead to initiate a covert bombing campaign from May 1970 against supplies and staging areas on the Cambodian border with South Vietnam.

Meanwhile, 'protective reaction' ('shoot when shot at') strikes increased in 1971 in response to attacks on US reconnaissance aircraft, with commanders in the field seeking means of stretching the rules so that attacks could extend beyond AAA sites to include MiG airfields and GCI

'Triple Nickel' F-4D-28-MC 65-0720 calls in to Phu Cat AB for fuel. The squadron was transferred to the 432nd TRW at Udorn on 1 June 1968, having become the first unit in South-east Asia to receive the latest version of USAF Phantom II when it re-equipped with F-4Ds in May 1967. The 555th TFS had previously flown F-4Cs with the 8th TFW from Ubon RTAFB between July 1966 and February 1968, claiming 19 MiG kills during this time (*Norm Taylor*)

radars. Officially, pilots were limited to 'hot pursuit' into the North's airspace of any MiGs that had overtly challenged them. Getting a MiG was taken seriously, although in Mike Cooper's view some of that was mainly an 'ego thing'.

MiG killer Brig Gen Dan Cherry recalled;

'We flew mostly recce escort over Route Pack (RP) I, close air support (CAS) with *Raven* FACs in Laos, *Laredo* Fast FAC in RP III, Laos and RP I, and an occasional strike mission around the DMZ. There was very little MiG activity prior to January 1972'.

Stu Maas added;

'Until we started seeing MiGs in the late autumn of 1971, most sorties were interdiction or CAS, not air-to-air. By the end of 1971 we were seeing more MiGs, even in Laos, chasing night-flying AC-130 gunships off their stations. By February 1972 we were into the night BARCAP business, and we shot down several MiGs, but the first daytime kills were on 16 April. We just didn't need to do ACM until then, so our skills were rusty and unwieldy. Doing full-blown air-to-air over a sophisticated enemy SA-2 net was another limiting factor. We expended great effort to get air supremacy by doing lots of SAM suppression before we got to the MiG-killing task.'

The anticipated invasion of South Vietnam began on 30 March 1972. Rather than re-deploying ground troops to the area, President Nixon decided to support the newly 'Vietnamized' forces of the south with increased airpower. Initially, 36th TFS F-4Ds from South Korea moved to Da Nang, while a series of *Constant Guard* deployments brought in F-4Es from the 334th TFS to Ubon from Seymour-Johnson AFB, the Eglin-based 58th TFS and Homestead-based 308th TFS to Udorn and F-4Ds from the four 49th TFW squadrons from Holloman AFB to the deserted Takhli RTAFB in May 1972. Other F-4 units came as additions or replacements as the conflict expanded.

Most of the incoming units were used to drive out the North Vietnamese Army invaders, leaving two veteran F-4 wings – the 8th TFW at Ubon RTAFB (concentrating on attack) and the 432nd TRW at Udorn RTAFB (with an air-to-air priority) – to deal with the impending war over the North.

B-52 attacks on targets in North Vietnam began with a 12-jet strike on 10 April – 20 F-4s were used to lay a chaff 'corridor' to mask the 'Buffs' from radar while other Phantom IIs flew MiGCAP. The bombing of Haiphong re-commenced on 16 April, and the first big MiG battle came out of an F-4 attack on an oil target near Hanoi that day. Three MiG-21s were destroyed by 432nd TRW jets. However, the first casualties of the renewed fighting had been sustained several weeks previously.

SECOND ROUND

January 1972 brought a steady increase in MiG challenges to US aircraft over Laos. F-4 squadrons engaged the VPAF fighters, but unreliable

469th TFS F-4Es shared in the outbreak of personal nose-art that enlivened South-east Asia-based aircraft in 1968-71, but this had largely vanished from Phantom IIs by 1972. F-4E-35-MC 67-0309 was assigned to Lt Col Erickson and 1Lt Williams, although neither they nor the jet were official recipients of a MiG kill confirmation. The star on *El Toro Bravo's* splitter plate was either a disallowed claim or a 'carry over' by a previous occupant of the cockpit. The aircraft appears to have suffered flak damage to its inboard wing pylon (*via C W Moggeridge*)

The 555th TFS commander's jeep wore this slogan. Col Ron Thurlow recalled that the vehicle was known to find its way into the Officers' Club during especially raucous celebrations (*Col R Thurlow*)

Triple Nickel

Largest distributor of Mig parts in SEA

missiles cost at least two early kill possibilities. However, on the night of 21 February the 555th TFS (transferred from the 8th TFW to the 432nd TRW in June 1968) got back into the MiG-slaying business after a four-year hiatus.

Maj Robert A Lodge and his WSO, 1Lt Roger Locher, were 'Falcon 62' in a two-ship MiGCAP, with a third F-4D flying 'radar trail' 5000 ft above them over Laos, 90 miles from Hanoi. Receiving vectors on two MiG-21s from the offshore radar fighter control ship *Red Crown*, they closed on them. 'Falcon 63' became separated from his element leader, but 1Lt Locher was able to identify the bandits as MiGs with his *Combat Tree* equipment and he locked onto one. Three AIM-7Es were fired, beginning at eleven miles range, and the first two detonated close enough to the MiG to cause a major explosion and fire.

Out of missiles (F-4s at that time usually carried an AN/ALQ-87 ECM pod in one of the forward missile wells), Maj Lodge broke off the engagement and dived away. Another pair of MiG-21s followed 'Falcon' flight, chasing them at low altitude and 500 knots for over 30 miles.

The following week 'Triple Nickel' F-4s made contact again. Lt Col Joe W Kittinger and 1Lt Leigh A Hodgdon were flying 'Falcon' MiGCAP with Maj R Carroll and Capt David L Harris over northern Laos on the night of 1 March 1972. At the time of their 1 March CAP mission, MiG interceptions were still relatively uncommon. As Leigh Hodgdon explained;

'I didn't have any other MiG contacts prior to that one. Although I did a lot of night flying, there wasn't much MiG hunting involved. We were on "Papa Alert" that night, and we were scrambled as one of two *Combat Tree* F-4Ds. Because of this, and the help of *Disco* EC-121s, we had a good chance of an intercept.'

The F-4 crews had been told to expect MiGs that might try to lure them into a fighter or SAM trap. Col Joe Kittinger takes up the story;

'The number two aircraft was heading for the tanker, which I had just departed from. I made a radio call that I was having trouble with transferring my fuel and would have to return to the tanker. This was a coded message to confuse the enemy, as we knew that they monitored all

Maj Robert Lodge and 1Lt Roger Locher destroyed all three of their MiGs with this F-4D-29-MC (65-0784), although the UD codes seen in this early January 1972 photograph had changed to OY by then. The jet was eventually shot down on 10 May with Maj Lodge still strapped into the cockpit. His knowledge of tactics and technology (particularly *Combat Tree*) made the thought of capture by the North Vietnamese intolerable to him, and he had told Roger Locher and others that he would not eject over enemy territory. Several of his former squadron members told the author that Lodge had decided to 'ride it in' and perish with his aircraft instead (*via Peter Schinkelshoek*)

of our radio transmissions. The controller on *Disco* recognised the bogus call and made the appropriate return call. I immediately dropped down to low level, skimming over the mountains as I flew towards the MiG. It was a very dark night, and I depended on my instruments and intimate knowledge of the terrain to avoid hitting the ground. 1Lt Hodgdon remained cool, performing his role professionally, even though we were flying at very high speed at night over mountains.'

Capts Olmsted and Volloy's F-4D MiG killer 66-0230 is seen in early 1972. It was shot down on 11 May that same year, and pilot, MiG killer Lt Col Joe Kittinger, was taken prisoner (*Patrick Martin via Peter Schinkelshoek*)

Combat Tree enabled the crew to identify the MiGs, which turned to follow two of the F-4s. They duly turned back into their pursuers, and Col Kittinger locked onto a MiG at a range of about 18 miles and shed the outboard fuel tanks. Leigh Hodgdon recalled;

'The one we shot down was head-on, which we could tell via the "Vc" circle (on the radar display) showing closing velocity. The in-range light illuminated at six miles, and we fired our first AIM-7E missile. We only had three Sparrows (one missile well being occupied by an ECM pod), and the first fell off the aircraft with motor ignition failure. The second one lit off and flew down at a 45-degree angle. Col Kittinger held the trigger down for another three seconds and the third Sparrow blasted off while he kept his steering circle centred. I calculated that the closing distance to the MiG was such that we were a fraction of a second away from the missile not arming in time to hit the MiG'.

Luckily, after a couple of small corrections during its five-second flight, the AIM-7 detonated and destroyed the MiG just as its pilot launched his missiles at Kittinger and Hodgdon's F-4D. The former immediately threw his fighter into a series of violent evasive manoeuvres, and to Leigh's relief, 'The missiles missed! What we didn't know – or didn't hear – was that there were three other MiGs after us from the side and, in one case, from nearly behind us. Our wingman yelled at us repeatedly about multiple MiGs, but we were too focused to hear him'.

Following this mission Leigh received a Silver Star – he eventually retired as a captain with three DFCs. Kittinger also received a Silver Star.

On 11 May 1972 – the day after one of the biggest fights of the war in which 11 MiGs were destroyed – Lt Col Kittinger's F-4D was downed by a MiG-21 that was in turn destroyed by his wingman, Capt Nichols. He became a PoW with his WSO, 1Lt William Reich, until March 1973, providing outstanding leadership to sustain the morale of his fellow prisoners. The F-4D used on his final Vietnam mission was 66-0230, a MiG killer for Capts 'Fredo' Olmsted and Gerald Volloy. His mount on the 1 March mission was F-4D 66-7463, which went on to destroy six MiGs altogether with five different crews.

BLACK BOXES

One factor in 66-7463's six kills was its high utilisation. As one of the handful of *Combat Tree*-equipped F-4Ds, it was always in demand as a flight lead aircraft. The jet was one of the original eight Block 29 F-4Ds to receive the APX-80 series equipment, as was the other F-4D (65-0784) used in these early 1972 fights. APX-80 gave the F-4 real BVR capability, which in turn meant that US crews had a significant technical advantage over their VPAF counterparts, since the latter could only employ limited to short-range IR missiles and gun armament at relatively close range.

The *Combat Tree* programme (originally called *Seek See*) had begun in 1968, and was spurred on by the covert acquisition of Soviet SRO-2 IFF transponders from Arab MiGs shot down by the Israelis during the Six Day War of June 1967. An APX-81 interrogator was combined with the APX-76, which interrogated the four IFF modes of friendly aircraft to avoid 'blue on blue' mishaps. Both were operated from a control unit on the lower left of the WSO's front instrument panel, and they shared an antenna attached to the aircraft's radar scanner. APX-81 could operate passively, receiving signals from the MiG's IFF, or actively by transmitting an interrogation signal to it. The resultant strobe indications appeared on the front and rear cockpit radar displays.

IFF identifications could be made at a range of up to 60 miles, which was way beyond the 20-mile detection range of F-4 radar. A WSO could then examine the two bar shape indications (known as 'grass') on his screen, which would tell him whether the target radar was 'squawking' an IFF mode and code that would identify itself as friend or foe. The second indication, based on the position of these two bars on his screen, showed him the approximate target location. As MiG-killing WSO Stan Pickett explained, 'The *Tree* equipment was totally operated from the rear cockpit. It was good for range and azimuth, but did not help in telling the target's altitude'.

The *Combat Tree* F-4Ds were assigned to the 3rd TFW at Kunsan AB, in South Korea, in March 1971, and four were transferred to the 432nd TRW nine months later. Secrecy surrounding the equipment initially meant that most crews were generally unfamiliar with the APX-80. Stu Maas recalled, 'I had never seen a *Tree* bird before we got the few that we had at Udorn. Most crews did their orientation in-theatre'.

Their success brought in the other four aircraft in January 1972, and it soon became *de rigeur* for at least two *Combat Tree* F-4Ds to be used in four-ship MiGCAPs wherever possible. Inevitably, this hastened their attrition, and five had been lost by August 1972. These F-4s had destroyed 12 MiGs by then, however, prompting the conversion of another batch of 20 F-4Ds. From 13 November these Phantom IIs began to be replaced by similarly-equipped, slatted-wing, *Rivet Haste* F-4Es, and the *Combat Tree* upgrade was eventually applied to all E-models.

One of its main advantages was that it made possible the elimination of 'blue on blue' long-range missile accidents, and the not infrequent chases of 'bandits' that turned out to be innocent F-4 strays. There were still rules of engagement that specified how far a *Combat Tree* jet had to be from known friendly aircraft before 'free fire' of its missiles at BVR targets could be sanctioned, however. The equipment also gave F-4 crews greater freedom to identify MiGs without having to rely on the sometimes-confusing information relayed from radar intelligence sources.

The next MiG kill of 1972 was also scored in a *Combat Tree* F-4D, (66-0230) being assigned to the 13th TFS/432nd TRW. Capts Frederick

Olmsted Jr and Gerald Volloy were leading 'Papa' flight on a 30 March alert scramble from Udorn, as the former explained;

'We had three birds on five-minute scramble. Our "sources" had indicated that the bad guys might make a run against an AC-130 gunship that evening, so the 432nd TRW decided to have three jets armed and ready to intervene.'

Capt Stu Maas was also (unexpectedly) on the mission as WSO in 'Papa 2';

'We were scheduled and parked as the deputy lead, call-sign "Papa 3", but "Papa 2" had a "hang fire start" (aborted engine starter cartridge) and so before he could re-start we blasted off in his place, leaving two non-flight lead qualified jets on the alert pad! It turned into a busy night. There were three VPAF aircraft airborne, types unknown, at the time, and the weather over RP I and II was bad. As we climbed out in the waning light on a north-easterly vector, GCI casually asked if we were "interested in running on a target". "Fredo" Olmsted's reply was "Yes", and we were off to the races. Flying through the "soup" in tight wingtip formation over the northern *Steel Tiger* area, we headed towards the Mu Gia Pass at about 18,000 ft, where we ran into our target.'

Fred Olmsted remembered, 'There was no VID since it was pitch black! We had flown through rain and cloud cover, directed by *Red Crown*. In fact, the Navy directed the entire low altitude night fight.'

Stu Maas continued;

'The lead WSO (Gerald Volloy) at first had no contact, but our ship did. I had a full-system lock-on, and was giving intercept instructions to Volloy, as well as preparing to fire. At a range of about seven miles the flight lead abruptly banked left and was "gone". We went on as "lost wingmen", and without the certainty of a target, or of the location of our flight lead, we held our fire. Shortly afterwards we heard "Fredo" and Volloy say they had fired a missile, and there was a distant explosion.

'My target was a single MiG-21, but at least three MiGs were up that night. Bobby Lodge also engaged a MiG at about the same time as we did, but without results.

'The entire fight took place below 1000 ft. Our radar altimeters were set at 1000 ft, and the red altitude alert light was constantly flashing on and off during the engagement. I remember Gerry saying, "Don't hit the ground, 'Fredo'!" over and over. We did get a missile launch, but due to the parameters we probably didn't give the missile too much of a chance. The motor ignited but we didn't see any impact or explosion.'

After Olmsted and Volloy's first AIM-7E was fired at a range of eight miles, two more were released. The last of these was at four miles, and this one produced a burgeoning fireball in the distance. *Red Crown*

Capt Keith Jones and Maj Barton Crews pose for the camera soon after their 8 May 1972 MiG kill. The F-4D behind them, borrowed for the photo shoot, was actually F-4D 66-0230, flown by Capts Olmsted and Volloy for their 30 March victory. The 13th TFS logo included a red '13' flanking a black panther's head. This aircraft has an adaptor rack for an ECM pod fitted into its forward port missile trough (*Lt Col K Jones*)

confirmed that the MiG radar trace had vanished. 'We then had to leave due to low fuel. We had made an afterburner dash to the coast to intercept the bandits, and with the entire fight at under 1000 ft, we had 'fumes' by the time the Navy confirmed our kill', recalled Fred Olmsted.

Stu Maas concluded;

'We independently turned south-west and headed for the tanker track. As we refuelled, we heard GCI vector other F-4s (Lodge and Locher were in one) into the area for engagements with more MiGs. None were engaged, although we heard later that one MiG ran out of fuel and crashed and another (rumoured to have been flown by a non-VPAF pilot) recovered successfully. I recall later sitting in the debrief and saying, "Always the bridesmaid and never the bride!" as Olmsted debriefed via 'phone to the generals in Saigon, who wanted to know about the action.'

Capt Maas got his chance to be 'the bride' on 16 April. When attacks on the Hanoi area resumed, Fred Olmsted was 'Basco' flight leader for an extra MiGCAP on an Alpha strike, with Stu Maas as his 'GIB', while 17 B-52s burned out oil tank farms near Hanoi, attracting over 100 SAMs. F-4s also struck petrol storage areas. 'Basco 1' flew multi-MiG killer 66-7463 on an 0830Z take-off from Udorn to a pre-strike orbit over the Laotian city of Ban Ban, where they awaited an F-4 strike flight. Maj Dan Cherry was flying 'Basco' 3 (F-4D 66-7550) with Capt Jeff Feinstein;

'As the minutes dragged on and the strike flight from Korat failed to show up, we began to think about our secondary CAP station to see what we could find in the area just south of Hanoi.'

As *Red Crown* checked their flight in, and they approached the North Vietnamese border, many non-specific SAM and MiG warning calls were passed to and between the F-4s. Sometimes this volume of incoming data could be confusing. 'There was a lot of UHF radio traffic, and we had to think quickly to maintain situational awareness and sort out the non-pertinent traffic', explained Stu Maas. Maintaining their orbit, they neared its northern extreme in a sky full of layered cloud decks and rain showers. Turning onto a heading of 340 degrees, 'Basco 1' picked up two MiGs on radar at a range of 20 nautical miles. Fred Olmsted recalled;

'*Red Crown* initially pointed us in the right direction, calling out "White and Blue bandits" (code-names for the MiG-19 and MiG-21). Stu then picked them up using the newly-installed *Tree* gear in my

This 13th TFS F-4D-30-MC (66-7550) was flown by Maj Dan Cherry and Capt Jeff Feinstein for the latter's first MiG kill, recorded on its splitter plate. All 'Basco' flight's ordnance loads were non-standard that day, as Brig Gen Cherry explained. 'Our flight was a last-minute add-on to the mission, so we had to take whatever was left over in terms of missiles, pods etc'. Capt Greg Crane ('Basco 4') had no AIM-9s, and although Dan Cherry had an ECM pod in a forward missile well, leader Olmsted's jet did not, and an SA-2 missile passed close to the flight during the mission. Three of the F-4s in the flight had three AIM-7Es apiece, although the jet crewed by Maj Cherry and Capt Feinstein had only two (*via C Moggeridge*)

aeroplane. Since I didn't understand how it worked, or trusted it, I
wasn't sure the bogeys weren't our
guys merely heading our way. Plus,
after nearly 300 missions where we
had to absolutely "VID" our targets,
I couldn't convince myself to shoot
BVR. But the two bogeys
"marched" right down the scope,
with Stu screaming in my headset to
"Kill 'em!" He was right. They were
two MiG-21s head-on to us. As it
turned out, there was also a "trailer"
MiG-21 coming up from the weeds
to act as shooter from behind.

'At that time the MiGs had
become much more aggressive, and they seemed more innovative in their
tactics. We were seeing different types of MiGs grouped together
(MiG-19s and MiG-21s), employing new tactics that saw a two-ship
trailed by a single "killer", or two-ships followed by a lower altitude two-
ship, and so on.'

Stu Maas explained;

'The MiG two-ship we met up with was called out as being "Bullseye
270/40" (40 mile west of Hanoi on a bearing of 270 degrees – all GCI
references to MiG bearings were relative to Hanoi, codenamed *Bullseye*).
We were south-west of *Bullseye*, having entered North Vietnam just north
of the "Fish's Mouth", and had just turned from our easterly heading to a
northerly one. A quick mental calculation indicated to me that there were
MiGs north of us, but they were not yet a threat. Keeping track of these
"players" was a team effort, and with up to ten flights on the same combat
frequency, it initially made inter-flight (and sometimes intra-cockpit)
communication difficult.

'I kept track of threats to us, as well as "friendlies" in our area, as I heard
them, mentally cataloguing them and quickly explaining to my pilot
what we ought to do next. In this specific case we jettisoned the external
tanks using a special manoeuvre that got them off without them colliding
with the airframe. We then began a shallow descent through the cloud
deck into clear air and picked up Mach.'

Dan Cherry remembered;

'Since there were some stringent limitations on jettisoning centreline
tanks, it was common practice to punch them off when they ran dry, if
combat was anticipated. We climbed, slowed down and punched off all
four tanks from the flight in unison.

'Col Bill McDonald, 308th TFS maintenance boss at Udorn,
explained to me that the centreline tanks were not combat tanks, but
really only ferry tanks, so a great many aircraft were damaged by the out-
of-parameter jettison of these tanks which would often roll along the
fuselage and over the stabilator, instead of falling away from the bird.

'As we approached Hoa Binh two things happened almost
simultaneously. Capt Stu Maas picked up a bogie on his radar at 20 miles.
About the same time our airborne controller called and directed us to

**Draped in essential survival gear,
including Raybans and moustache,
Capt Fred Olmsted looks thirsty
while Maj Dan Cherry gets the beer.
Reflecting on the 13th TFS's
contribution to the mission on 16
April 1972, Brig Gen Cherry recalled,
'We had flown an entire mission
with only the fuel we had taken off
with, shot down two MiGs and done
it without any help from radar
controllers. That was fairly unusual,
and the four-minute length of the
engagement was pretty rare too'.
Both kills were accomplished with
AIM-7s, which was considered by
'Fredo' Olmsted to have been 'a
good weapon for the time. I fired
nine and got three hits. This was
considered acceptable. The
"switchology" to prepare for a
launch was a bit cumbersome,
which made a lot of our guys prefer
the "point and shoot" AIM-9. But it
sure got everybody's attention when
one of those "great white sharks"
was fired into a big dogfight!'
(via Fred Olmsted)**

proceed to a new orbit point down by the DMZ. Since we had contact, and an engagement seemed imminent, we disregarded their instructions and turned to put the bogies on our nose.'

Stu Maas continued;

'"Basco" has bandits on the nose, 21 (nautical miles)" was my first call on UHF. I did have *Combat Tree* "grass" at the bottom of the scope, indicating azimuth and presence, but just "grass" was not good enough. I soon had a full *Tree* indication ("grass" just above and just below a radar return at range and azimuth), and at 11 nautical miles I called out "Basco on the nose, 11". We were fast, with full systems in range lock, good tracking and closure. I told "Fredo" to "shoot, shoot, shoot" at seven miles. With rules of engagement allowing a full-lock on and *Tree* ID, we were authorised to shoot BVR, but "Fredo" did not'.

Dan Cherry recalled that they had permission to attack with only a *Tree* ID, 'But we pre-briefed a flight procedure requiring a visual ID before attacking'. In any case, as Stu Maas described it;

'In seconds the fight was on. Four clean, roaring Phantom IIs versus two MiG-21s. When "Fredo" visually ID'd them, they were slightly high at "11 o'clock", going in the opposite direction. I believe they were surprised to see us, as later intel indicated that they were running on a target further south than us – a single *Iron Hand* EB-66 that we had seen and passed about 15-20 miles further south. The MiGs' reaction was to begin a slight climbing left turn and split. The wingman probably got "spat out" by the lead MiG's abrupt left turn. "Fredo", with Capt Steve Cuthbert in a fighting wing position, worked on one side, while Dan Cherry and Capt Greg Crane worked the other. I recall checking Steve's position once during the first seconds of the engagement, and he was "right in there" at my "eight o'clock", about 800-1000 ft out.

'"Fredo" never lost sight of that lonesome MiG. I think it was the wingman, because his turn eased off and he began a slight descent, indicating to me that he had lost sight of the "engagers" and his partner.

Although it is heavily laden with Mk 82 bombs, this F-4D still carries a pair of AIM-7E-2s for self-defence. The missile was developed in response to the poor results achieved by earlier AIM-7D/E variants during Operation *Rolling Thunder*, when 260 Sparrows were fired but only 20 kills were confirmed. Many of them were launched at low altitudes, inside range parameters or in salvoes against manoeuvring targets, severely reducing the missiles' chances of success. The AIM-7E-2 could be launched at shorter ranges (1500 ft, compared with 3300 ft for the standard AIM-7E) against a non-manoeuvring target flying at the same speed. It also tracked targets better and detonated more reliably (*Doug Malloy*)

With a full radar lock and in a slight left turn, ten degrees nose low, we shot our first AIM-7. I watched it through the side quarter-panel of the canopy as it guided towards the MiG's right wing-tip. Then I watched AIM-7 number two's contrail sail off to heaven at "two o'clock high". It never guided. Number three – our last AIM-7 – flew perfectly, colliding just behind the MiG's canopy as we maintained our descending left turn.

'Generally, we could shoot all the AIM-7s we had aboard at a target aircraft without hesitation, but with a "shoot/brief look/shoot" pattern, if the missile looked like it was guiding, we'd hold off with the next one. If the first indications were that there might be a tracking problem, the next missile was launched.'

Dan Cherry, leading the second element, recalled;

'After using "Basco 1's" *Combat Tree* for the initial contact and identification, Stu maintained his radar contact and called them out as we closed to five miles and then picked them up visually. We saw two silver MiGs about 5000 ft higher than we were. We cranked it around, trying to keep the MiGs in sight. I was on the outside of the turn, so I fell behind. Half way through the turn my wingman called a third MiG – a camouflaged MiG-21 – at "12 o'clock" to me, and climbing into position behind Olmsted's element. The VPAF had apparently been setting a trap, using the silver MiGs as bait. The camouflaged MiG had been at low altitude, and as we started our turn to chase the silver MiGs, he had climbed, hoping to roll in behind us. I rolled out of my turn and headed directly for him. He turned hard left away from me and into a cloud.'

Thinking that they may have lost their potential target, "Basco 3" followed the MiG into the cloud for some time, pulling up and out of it only at the possibility of unseen SAMs rising from below. As they turned back towards Capt Olmsted's element, Greg Crane saw the camouflaged MiG above them in a climbing turn. Dan Cherry continues;

'I went to max afterburner and pulled around to go after him. As I pulled the nose of the Phantom II up, I had a beautiful set-up for a Sidewinder shot. The sun was more or less behind us, and there was nothing out in front except the MiG. I pulled the nose out in front of him as I selected "heat" (AIM-9) and pulled the trigger. Nothing happened. The perfect shot and my aeroplane was broken! When I returned to base the AIM-9s were gone, but there was no indication from my wingman or in the cockpit that they functioned properly. We did have serious reliability problems then, probably because of the missiles' age, and all the uploading and downloading that had gone on for several years.'

Cherry thought that his AIM-9s may have been knocked of when he jettisoned his wing-tanks. Bill McDonald explained;

'The AIM-9s had to be handled with kid gloves as they were sensitive to mishandling, and one had to be cautious about the seeker head glass

The 13th TFS's Maj Dan Cherry and Capt Fred Olmsted go through the motions of their 16 April 1972 combat. Behind them is F-4D 66-7463 (Olmsted's 'Basco 1'), armed with AIM-7E-2 Sparrows and a pair of AIM-9Es (*USAF via Col R Thurlow*)

This 523rd TFS F-4D-32-MC (66-8734) was among the 405th FW Phantom IIs that deployed to the 432nd TRW in April 1972, and it had acquired OY codes by the time Capts John Markle and Steve Eaves used it for their 10 May 1972 MiG kill (*via Peter Schinkelshoek*)

domes so as not to scratch or break them. We didn't keep AIM-9s uploaded on TAC birds overnight as a precautionary rule. However, the AIM-7s were generally kept up in their fuselage locations.'

As Dan Cherry's target MiG entered a diving spiral to try and escape a second missile, Jeff Feinstein was unable to lock it on radar. Greg Crane duly called that he was taking over the lead;

'I rolled around him into fighting wing formation as Greg lined up the MiG in his sights and fired his missiles. His first weapon malfunctioned and fell away, and the next round went into a corkscrewing spiral and missed'.

They were fired without a radar lock, but still, as Stu Maas observed, the missiles 'did guide Dan's eyes to the MiG, since he didn't have a visual tally'. The final AIM-7 guided well, but 'just prior to impact, the MiG driver broke hard and the Sparrow went right by his tail without exploding'. The MiG's turn meant that he quickly bled off energy, and both crews were determined to nail him even though their only remaining missiles were Cherry's two AIM-7s. 'Even if my Sparrows didn't fire, I would have had to chase him until I reached "bingo" fuel and then turn for home.'

Greg Crane had the same idea, and chased the bandit in full afterburner, although his radio had failed and he couldn't hear 'Basco 3's' call that he was taking back the element lead role. With Greg's jet ahead of them, Cherry and Feinstein could not risk taking an AIM-7 shot. However, their Phantom II was a bit faster than Crane's, and they soon got level with him. Dan Cherry described the climax of the chase;

'I called Jeff and told him, "I've got the sight right on the MiG. Lock him up". He did, and the analogue indication popped out on the edge of the gunsight indicating a good radar lock-on. I clamped down on the trigger again, never expecting the missile to come off, but suddenly, "Whoosh!" That big AIM-7 smoked out in front of us as we accelerated through 500 knots in a descending turn to the right. It did a big barrel roll, and at first I thought it would miss him as it appeared to be going too far out in front of him.

'The missile impacted on the MiG about 4000 ft ahead of "Basco 3". The explosion blew the right wing off the MiG, and it immediately went into a hard spiral, trailing fire and smoke. The pilot ejected and his 'chute opened right in front of me – I turned hard left to make sure I didn't fly

through it. We were close to supersonic, with the afterburners cooking, and I know we weren't more than 30 ft away from him when we passed.'

Dan fleetingly noticed the pilot's black flying suit and white parachute with one red stripe on it.

'By this time we were low on fuel, and I had but one thought at that point – let's get out of here before more MiGs show up.'

Heading back to Udorn at treetop level, they hoped to find a tanker so that there would be fuel 'to show off a bit when we got back'. A shortage of tankers prevented this, and they arrived at Udorn with less than 1000 lbs of fuel.

16 April also yielded a third kill, this time for an F-4D of the 523rd TFS on Temporary Duty (TDY) with the 432nd TRW. Stu Maas explained;

'As the entire "Basco" flight headed home, and the celebration (champagne and cigars all round), we were chased out by a MiG. Coming off the Udorn "Papa Alert" pad was a flight of F-4s, one of which

was crewed by Capts Jim Null and Mike Vahue. We passed each other, and shortly thereafter they downed the MiG.'

The 523rd TFS had only re-grouped at Udorn a week previously after being divided up between the three 'in-theatre' bases following its 7 February deployment from Clark AB. The 523rd was the Thirteenth Air Force's only operational unit at Clark, and its crews theorised that a senior officer at the base had wanted to get in some combat flying. In fact theatre indoctrination had begun before Christmas 1971, and Mike Vahue was one of the first four aircrew sent to Udorn for this. Sadly, fellow 523rd WSO 1Lt Dan Poynor was killed on a *Falcon* FAC mission over the Plain of Jars with 555th TFS pilot Capt Leo Thomas in *Combat Tree* F-4D 66-0237 on 19 December 1971, and the plan to do local orientation for the rest of the unit was abandoned until the whole unit deployed.

On 16 April Mike and Jim almost did not make the alert scramble that resulted in their kill as their aircraft had been 'stolen' to make up a large strike force. 555th TFS pilot Mike Cooper explained that as Ops Officer, 'if we ran out of aeroplanes we would skim them off the "Papa Alert" pad'. Having at last located serviceable F-4s in the revetments and got airborne, the crews' problems weren't over, as Mike Vahue explained;

'I had a cockpit problem. Back-seaters carry so much junk – maps, checklists etc – that something got in the way of my radar cursor control stick so that I couldn't get the cursor on the MiGs for a radar lock-on, so we lost them. We came round again and Jim cleared our wingman, Gary Lorenz, to shoot. I don't know why – maybe he had a switching problem – but all his missiles fell off. Then we got a vector, which I think was from *Teaball* (centralised intelligence location at Nakhon Phanom RTAFB) that gave us the info we needed. We came up behind the MiGs' "six o'clock". We were "in the weeds" then at less than 1000 ft, headed for Hanoi. We had all the parameters we needed, and Jim loosed off all three AIM-7Es at the second MiG.'

The second missile detonated by proximity fuse near the left side of the silver MiG, its expanding-rod warhead tearing off its rear fuselage and causing an intense fire. The MiG rolled over and hit the ground. No parachute was seen. Intel reported another hostile aircraft orbiting in the same area, but 'Papa 3' could not do any more.

Jim Null (centre) and Mike Vahue (partially hidden, second from right) discuss their aerial victory with other 523rd TFS members on 16 April 1972. Jim and Mike almost missed the alert scramble that yielded their kill, as the latter explained. 'We were sitting "Papa Alert" with four birds on 5-10 minute alert. "Papa 1" and "2" had been scrambled earlier for a weather recce of the target area for the big strike that day. They scrambled us as "Papa 3", with Gary Lorenz as "Papa 4", and we ran out from the crew area, but we didn't have any aeroplanes! They had taken them for the heavy strike too. They needed 80-100 aeroplanes, and two didn't check out, so they came and got ours. I was just about to go back and finish my omelette, but Jim went up and down the flightline looking for a couple of birds. He talked to the command post and they said they wanted us in the air, so if we could find some F-4s configured for MiGCAP we should go and get them. Jim found a couple and we scrambled 45 minutes late. We went out to the north-east, and right away we got vectors from *Red Crown*. There were two silver MiG-21s that went past right above us, and so the fight began' (*Mike Vahue*)

'We couldn't go after the second MiG because were out of AIM-7s (one missile trough had an ECM pod in it), and all we had were AIM-4Ds (still installed on Clark F-4Ds at that time). They had a good guidance system but didn't have much of a punch. We were also getting low on gas and heading for Hanoi at over Mach 1.'

A fourth AIM-7 might have been more use than an ECM pod at that time, since SAM and AAA threats were fairly infrequent. In any case, as Mike Vahue commented;

'We all had RHAW/ECM gear but mostly didn't use it. It made a lot of noise and it didn't discriminate enough. It gave us vectors all over the place, all the time and it could be very distracting. Usually, we turned the volume down to the point where we could hardly hear it. Our cues were mostly visual – we could see the SA-2 launch so the ECM gear was just a pain, particularly with so much radio traffic coming from 80 to 90 aeroplanes on the same frequency. One chatterbox and radio discipline was dead – no-one could talk! We had a squadron frequency – UHF 3030 with the code-word "Winchester" – that we could go to.'

As April went by, the 'heavies' to Hanoi increased, with F-4s configured mainly for bombing. Udorn was regularly launching combined missions with Ubon of up to 130 bombers, plus MiGCAPs and support aircraft. Increasingly, the crews felt that Washington was trying to win the war via the sortie rate.

For the 523rd TFS crews accustomed to sitting nuclear alert on a monthly rota in Taiwan (with potential targets in China), or air defence alert, their Vietnam deployment involved continued alert on a three-week schedule with the other Udorn units (13th and 555th TFSs), but mainly a variety of attack tasks. Among these were LORAN bombing and LGB missions. For the latter, Udorn F-4s dropped 2000-lb Paveway I weapons, and Ubon Phantom IIs provided the laser capability with their AN/AVQ-10 Pave Knife pods.

Sixty 8th TFW F-4Ds received the *Pave Phantom* updates from 1967 onwards, including AN/ARN-92 LORAN navigation aids. These aircraft were still flying from Ubon in 1972, including this particular aircraft from the 25th TFS. LORAN bombing wasn't accurate enough to use near friendly troops, as MiG killer Mike Vahue explained. 'Orbiting over a set of coordinates and bombing from 15,000-18,000 ft, you had no idea of wind directions or strength'. If the target was at all uncertain, the bombs had to be "pickled" into a safe dump area, as crews hated to land with them aboard'. Vahue once had to land back at base with 12 Mk 82s aboard, and he finally stopped his F-4 just 40 ft short of the runway's end (*Leigh Hodgdon*)

The MiG kill scoreboard in the 555th TFS crew lounge in 1973. This was later transferred to Luke AFB (*Col R Thurlow*)

LINEBACKER LAUNCHED

8 May 1972 brought President Nixon's announcement that the bombing of North Vietnam would be resumed, together with the mining of its ports. Air power had apparently stopped the North Vietnamese take-over of the south, and the next US objective was to destroy the vast military supplies stored in the North that might be used for another invasion. Airfields, SAM sites and other previously off-limits targets were included. Operation *Linebacker I* began 24 hours later, but the MiG kills re-commenced the very day the President delivered his statement. They began with the first shoot-down of a VPAF MiG-19.

Fifty-four MiG-19S 'Farmers' (actually Chinese licence-built Shenyang J-6) fighters were delivered in 1968-69 to equip the 925th FR, which also flew MiG-17F 'Fresco-Cs'. The unit's MiG-19 pilots eventually claimed five Phantom IIs destroyed (only three were admitted by US forces), but the *Farmer* had a high accident rate, and at least ten fell to F-4s. By October 1972 there were insufficient serviceable aircraft left to continue operational use.

The MiG-19's first combat engagement took place on 8 May when two flights were positioned at opposite ends of their Yen Bai base to prevent strikes on the Thac Ba hydroelectric plant. The VPAF pilots encountered the incoming 'Galore' MiGCAP flight as it headed south towards Yen Bai from its CAP point orbit. The F-4Ds split into two elements, with Maj Barton P Crews and WSO Capt Keith W Jones (of the 13th TFS) flying as element lead in 'Galore 3'. Capt Jones reconstructed the combat;

'I had *Combat Tree*, and had detected a blip on our nose. I told Bart, but didn't call it out to the flight leader because I lost the blip and could not be sure of its validity. Moments later another flight member called "Bogies at '12 o'clock' – appear to be friendly". Bart then spotted them and radioed, "They are NOT friendly!" The lead MiG passed under us, slightly right, and initiated a left turn – very strange, because a right turn was needed to get behind us. I don't believe he saw us, or, like the rest of us in the flight, it was his first ever engagement and he, like many of us, was prone to beginner's mistakes. At any rate, Bart made no mistakes. He turned hard right into the trailing MiG and told me to get a lock-on.

'Unfortunately, when the engagement began, we were at a point in our orbit where our airspeed was lower than ideal, and Bart's hard manoeuvring took the aircraft close to a stall, causing it to shudder significantly. This prevented me from managing the radar tracking handle well enough to achieve the lock-on. I told Bart, and he said "Go boresight". I did, and this "froze" the radar antenna looking straight ahead, so that if Bart could manoeuvre to get the MiG on our nose, he could use the "auto-acquisition" switch on the throttle to get a lock-on.

'He masterfully achieved everything, but could not get the lock-on since the "auto-acquisition" feature had failed. He fired an AIM-7 without a lock-on, then made a hard turn toward the lead MiG, which was by then manoeuvring behind us, but he couldn't get a tracking solution on him either. I saw a yellow 'chute go by on the left, but didn't see an occupant. I assumed it was a MiG drag 'chute, maybe deployed intentionally for quick deceleration to cause us to overshoot. As the second MiG got behind us and began firing, Bart, with insufficient airspeed to out-manoeuvre him, dived into cloud and we escaped. Neither Bart nor I heard "Gip" Magill's ("Galore 4") radio call "That's a kill!"

'After landing, several squadron members met us to congratulate us on our kill. I laughed, saying that the yellow 'chute (the supposed "verification" of the kill) was a MiG drag 'chute. Later, when Magill and his WSO Tim Holland told us they had both observed the MiG go into a downward spiral, I happily assumed I was wrong, and that the MiG pilot had bailed out after losing control while dodging our missile. That night Seventh Air Force confirmed our kill through intelligence channels, and some eight hours after the engagement, Bart and I celebrated.'

The VPAF maintained that the MiG-19 pilot, Nguyen Hong Son (known as 'Son A') tried to jettison his wing tanks, selected the wrong lever and triggered his brake parachute instead. The 'chute allegedly ripped away and was instantly identified by Nguyen Ngoc Tiep, leader of the other MiG element, as evidence of an American pilot ejecting! At any rate, the kill was officially awarded to Maj Crews and Capt Jones, and another star appeared on their F-4D, 66-7463.

The other MiGCAP flight, 'Oyster', was led Maj Bob Lodge and WSO Capt Roger Locher (555th TFS). It entered the arena at the rear of the strike force a few minutes after 'Galore' flight's tussle, and was directed by *Red Crown* to aid an F-4 flight that was under attack by MiG-21s near Yen Bai. That fight soon ended, however, so the controller re-directed them towards another MiG flight that was heading in from the east. Capt Locher got a positive *Combat Tree* ID and his flight turned to engage the MiG-21s. He acquired one on radar and closed on it, but then noticed a trailing MiG-21 at his 'one o'clock' that was closer than the lead MiG.

Perhaps confirming the prevalent VPAF belief that USAF pilots preferred to attack wingmen rather than flight leaders, Lodge locked on to this second MiG, approaching at Mach 1.4 from a low position into its pilot's blind spot. At a range of 4500 ft, with 20 degrees angle off, he ripple-fired a pair of AIM-7Es as the MiG reversed its turn to the left. The first missile hit its right wing, closely followed by the impact of the second Sparrow on the fuselage centre. The 921st FR MiG-21 began to disintegrate, and its pilot (possibly Vo Si Giap) climbed away hard and received an order to eject. Bob Lodge, who had moved a step closer to his avowed goal of acedom, reported that he passed close to a pilot below a yellowish parachute as he egressed through the area at low altitude.

Mike Cooper went after the second MiG-21 in the flight after observing Lodge's missiles destroy the leader;

'Bob had a real high overtake speed on the MiGs, so I picked up the lead and made a couple of turns with the second guy. I expended at least three AIM-4Ds on the second MiG, plus the two AIM-7s that I was carrying. The AIM-4Ds didn't work, and the continuous wave illuminator for the

AIM-7s failed so that they went awry. He rolled out straight and level at 15,000 ft, apparently waiting for the inevitable end, but I was parked 600 ft behind him with nothing to shoot!'

Future ace Capt Steve Ritchie was Mike Cooper's wingman that day, and he was the next to destroy a MiG 48 hours later in a historic battle that cost Bob Lodge his life. Three more MiGs fell to 432nd TRW crews, one of which was Maj Lodge's third, and final, victim.

CAPS AND 'CHAFFERS'

As the primary counter-air wing in-theatre, Udorn's 432nd TRW coupled its strike and reconnaissance tasks with a variety of CAP functions. All were designed to protect the strike elements, rather than hunt MiGs. As *Linebacker* developed and B-52 attacks on North Vietnam increased, it became necessary to protect the F-4 flights that dropped chaff to form 15-minute airborne 'corridors' of metal foil strips that degraded enemy SAM and AAA radars. Up to 20 F-4s accompanied each raid, dropping Mk 129 chaff bombs at slow speed in straight and level flight formations that were vulnerable to MiGs. Bill McDonald recalled;

'The chaff configurations were changed several times until the tech reps brought the dispenser on line that would effectively provide chaff for the corridor. Before that, there were several jury-rigged efforts, including stuffing speed-brake wells with chaff. There were plenty of efforts to try and "tune" the dispersal rate so as to gain the maximum radar return, resulting in the length of some chaff strips being increased'.

Chaff flights needed three or four MiGCAP flights per mission. Increasingly, these were provided by the 432nd TRW, while the 'chaffers' came either from the 8th TFW at Ubon or TDY squadrons. Udorn also mounted MiGCAPs over the target areas, and one or two more to cover the egress of the strikers. These were timed to arrive over the egress routes about ten minutes before the strikers began to make their way out. They could also relieve other fuel-thirsty CAP F-4s, and cover the post-strike reconnaissance RF-4Cs. Smaller barrier CAP (BARCAP) flights, often comprising two Phantom IIs, could also be placed between potential threats and US tanker, surveillance or jamming aircraft.

Col Cooper pointed out another aspect of their role;

Udorn RTAFB, looking north-east (*USAF via Col R Thurlow*)

'Once the "chaffers" had begun their chaff runs they were self-defending, so we would normally break off and run a MiG sweep up the Red River, maybe to Yen Bai. This was a standard tactic for the 555th and 13th TFSs.'

Finally, there were the crucial escort flights (usually two F-4 four-ships) that accompanied the strike force, breaking out to engage any MiGs that threatened the strike armada. As in *Rolling Thunder*, one was usually situated near the front of the 'procession', while a second flight tailed it at higher altitude to catch MiGs attacking from the rear.

On 10 May one MiGCAP flight ('Oyster') was responsible for all three of the day's Air Force kills. In all, 120 USAF aircraft were launched, including 32 F-4 bombers, eight 'chaffers' and 28 air-to-air configured F-4s. 'Oyster' (555th TFS) and 'Balter' (13th TFS) flights were the pre-strike support MiGCAPs, entering North Vietnamese airspace at 0920 hrs ahead of a huge strike formation as it headed for the Paul Doumer Bridge and Yen Bai railyard. En route, two 'Balter' F-4Ds aborted with systems problems, and 'Oyster 4' (1Lt Tommy Feezel and Capt Larry 'Doc' Pettit) lost their radar capability, but stayed with the flight.

The 'Oysters', in a plan devised by Bob Lodge, were established at low altitude to BARCAP north-west of Hanoi in the hope that they could catch any MiGs heading for 'Balter', flying 22,000 ft higher. The *Disco* EC-121D had earlier reported MiGs rising from Kep air base, some distance to the north-east, and an hour later *Red Crown* (manned by Chief Radarman Larry Nowell on USS *Chicago*) reported four separate MiG elements airborne. These MiGs repeatedly flew towards the oncoming Americans and then drew back. At 0942 hrs, they began to close on the area where the two F-4 MiGCAPs were flying their figure-of-eight orbits.

Maj Lodge turned his 'low' flight and climbed slightly to meet them, while his WSO got MiG indications on *Combat Tree* – both he and the element leader (Capts Ritchie and DeBellevue) were in *Combat Tree* F-4Ds. As 1Lt John Markle (pilot of 'Oyster 2') explained;

'It made sense that the lead aircraft would have the benefit of *Combat Tree*, if available, the best radar and the most armament. The next priority would be the number 3 aircraft as element leader, while numbers 2 and 4 would receive the lowest priority. It would have been very unlikely that someone other than the lead would have the *Combat Tree* resource due to availability. It really was an advantage, but one that was used in concert with GCI and other resources'.

Certainly, as 'Oyster 2', Markle's F-4 was fairly lightly armed;

'Steve Eaves (WSO) and I had two AIM-7s and one AIM-4D. All jets had jamming pods in the forward missile wells, and three external tanks'.

As the first F-4s into the area, 'Oyster' had the advantage of a 'missiles free' situation without the visual ID requirement, and at 13 nautical missiles Roger Locher watched his 'in range' light come on and waited for the allowable steering area (ASE) circle on his radar screen to start contracting. Maj Lodge then fired a single AIM-7 at a range of eight nautical miles as his F-4D blasted ahead at Mach 1.4. The missile climbed and tracked, but detonated early when its motor burned out. He fired a second and saw the missile climbing at 20 degrees towards its still-invisible target. A large fireball implied success, which was confirmed as 'Oyster 1' passed a disintegrating MiG-21 minus its left wing and pilot.

Markle and Eaves got the second MiG when they fired both their AIM-7s from a position 600 yards off Lodge's right wing. John Markle;

'We were trained to fire two missiles against each target, since the reliability issues with the AIM-7 were built into our training – fire two, with a 50 per cent possibility of a good launch. It is interesting to note that both Lodge and Ritchie were Fighter Weapons School (FWS) graduates, and thus had the confidence to fire single Sparrows that worked. Both were certainly tactically more "savvy", and they better understood the concept of weapons conservation when needed. Most of us were just out of RTU, where we were taught the "world-wide way" of using the F-4, and its weapons. Another factor was that AIM-7s were relatively plentiful and MiG shots were rare.'

'Oyster 2's' first missile apparently suffered motor failure, but the second climbed and struck its target, sending the third MiG in the flight tumbling out of control as its right wing separated. Maj Lodge, determined to get another kill, set off after the lead MiG, while the second 'Oyster' element pursued the fourth jet. Ritchie fired two AIM-7E-2s from 6000 ft. The first guided well, but passed close under the MiG-21 without detonating, while the second generated a lurid orange fireball and a mass of debris where the fighter had been. Chuck DeBellevue's sighting of a yellow parachute as they passed confirmed the first of a string of MiGs for he and Steve Ritchie. He yelled, '"Oyster Three's" a splash!'

Bob Lodge was within seconds of destroying a fourth MiG-21 when the four MiG-19S fighters of No 2 Flight, 925th FR unexpectedly entered the fight. Moments after take-off, Nguyen Manh Tung climbed to a position behind 'Oyster 1', whose crew were focused on their target, which had almost collided with their F-4 and was by then in afterburner and pulling away just ahead of them. Sadly, their Phantom II had no gun aboard for what could have been an easy shot. Initially, Tung overshot the 'Oyster' lead on their left side, and 1Lt Markle yelled a warning to reverse right. Lodge, having established the correct distance for a missile launch, remained 'padlocked' to his MiG and fired an AIM-7E-2.

Further warnings from 'Oyster' 2 couldn't shift Lodge and Locher as a stream of 30 mm shells from the MiG-19 leader's three NR-30 cannon headed for their Phantom II. Locher noticed their MiG-21 accelerating away unscathed by their missile as their own aircraft seemed to slow after what felt like a mid-air collision from the shell strikes. Tung fired again. The F-4's hydraulics were disabled and its right engine seemed to have exploded. Fire surged forward through the aircraft, filling the cockpit with smoke and toasting Locher's rear canopy to orange opacity.

Turning on full oxygen as the jet descended through 8000 ft, he advised his pilot to eject, but Lodge refused and told Locher to punch out. In desperation, Locher ejected himself with the aircraft inverted, shortly before it shattered on the ground with Lodge still aboard.

In a bizarre twist, Nguyen Manh Tung, returning to base elated after shooting down Lodge's F-4, ran out of fuel on final approach, landed too fast and over-ran the end of the runway. His MiG flipped over and he died in the conflagration.

Moments later, the MiG-19s struck again when Pham Hung Son led the 925th FR's first section in an attack on Lt Col Rollins' 'Harlow' MiGCAP (covering an F-4D LGB strike). The number four F-4E, flown by Capts Jeff Harris and Dennis Wilkinson, was wingman for the MiG-killing team of Bart Crews and Keith Jones that day. As Lt Col Jones recounted;

'Mike McCarthy, the WSO in "Harlow 2", was the squadron wit, famous for keying his radio switch and saying "quack, quack" to remind his flight that they were sitting ducks for SAMs while on MiGCAP, but he was also an astute airman.

Armament specialists prepare a 'great white shark' AIM-7E-2, still without fins, for uploading to an F-4E. The mobile shelter behind them kept some of the monsoon rain out of the cockpits of the Phantom IIs parked in the open on the vast flightlines at Ubon and Udorn (*Col Bill F McDonald*)

'Our first indication of the MiG's presence was McCarthy's crisp call, "'Harlow 3', you've got a MiG on your ass!" We were in a right bank, so I immediately looked to the right, saw "Harlow 4" tucked into a perfect fighting wing position, and the MiG planted behind him. I called "break" over the live interphone and Bart banked left as hard as he could. We never saw "Harlow 4" again.

'It was struck by 30 mm shells from Son's MiG and plunged to earth with its crew aboard. The MiG then vanished. McCarthy called "Harlow 3" (rather than "4") because it was standard practice to radio the element leader, not an individual flight member when the elements were separated for mutual support. Also, McCarthy could not have discerned which F-4 was the MiG's target, although this didn't matter since "Harlow 4" would not manoeuvre independently – it would follow our manoeuvre. If McCarthy had not made the call, the MiG pilot would, in all probability, have shot us down too. I believe Bart and I owe our lives to that call, although it was tragically seconds too late to save Jeff and Denny. I must reluctantly conclude that the MiG pilot deserved credit for astonishing cleverness and ability.'

The loss of Robert Lodge was a severe one for the 432nd TRW. As Weapons and Tactics Officer, he had initiated many important new approaches. John Markle had flown with him on four-hour night MiGCAPs in early 1972, blocking MiGs from harassing the AC-130 gunships over Laos;

'Bob and Roger Locher were innovative in their attempts to both provide proper mission coverage and give the MiGs some incentive to fly at night. We tried erroneous radio transmissions, claiming weapons systems or aircraft problems, in the hope of duping the VPAF into thinking we were crippled. At times we tried flying close formation to create a radar image of a single aircraft on CAP.

'In March 1972 Bob was instrumental in the planning and coordination of the "protective reaction" strikes into RP I, deemed "illegal" but proved legitimate when the North Vietnamese invaded the South. It was my impression that Bob was *the* force behind these actions in support of Seventh Air Force/CC directives. He also utilised the LORAN equipment in many ways. One I recall was to use the coordinates of a point offset from a predetermined target to establish proper lateral spacing for a desired dive angle. When over that point, you simply varied the altitude for the different angle – e.g. 10,000 ft AGL for a 30-degree dive, or 15,000 ft for a 45-degree dive, etc. The result was very accurate dive angles, and better deliveries'.

The low altitude CAP orbit that Lodge used on 10 May was a favourite;

'He used terrain masking well during our MiGCAPs outside the Hanoi area. We would normally stay below the hills, receiving *Bullseye* calls from airborne sources. When we needed to, we would pop up to update our position and receive information from *Red Crown*. Outside Hanoi, the AAA or SAM threat was low. This also favoured us for a look-up shot with either radar or heat-seeking missiles, both of which preferred this upward angle of fire.'

Bill McDonald dined with Lodge three nights before his shoot-down. 'He happened to mention offhandedly, and with some candour, that he felt he could never be taken prisoner since he knew too much'. He had also told Roger Locher of his intentions. Although Lodge was a modest, intense man who never posed as a potential ace, it was widely believed that he was the Air Force's best bet to achieve that honour.

His untimely death after three kills left Capt Locher as the highest scorer, but in early July the focus switched to Steve Ritchie after his third kill. In any case, Locher spent 23 days after 10 May evading capture in North Vietnam. Uninjured in his ejection, he lived on the meagre fruits of the forest in his attempt to walk 90 miles to high ground, and the possibility of rescue. When he first landed, he made a rescue beeper signal but forgot to press the 'transmit' button, so potential rescuers had no idea whether he had survived.

Narrowly avoiding detection on several occasions, Locher grew weaker, but managed to trek as far as the Red River, which he would have attempted to cross in order to reach higher ground. He became aware of aircraft nearby, and tried another radio transmission using his call-sign, 'Oyster One Bravo' (flight lead, back-seater). John Madden was among the 'Triple Nickel' pilots flying close to Locher's position near Yen Bai;

'I was on a mission with Steve Ritchie leading when Locher came up on the radio and said, "Say, you guys. Can anyone come and pick me up?" We shut down all missions except rescue and got him out. I was at Udorn ramp when the rescue helicopter came in.'

The first rescue attempt, deep in North Vietnam was frustrated when a MiG-21 happened to pass the helicopters and A-1 *Sandy* escort, fortunately without attacking. Gen J W Vogt (Seventh Air Force Commander) sanctioned a second attempt, despite the high probability of losing aircraft, in order to show commitment to his aircrews. In all, 119 aircraft were scheduled for the operation, including 16 F-4s to ground the MiGs at Yen Bai airfield, and another 16 to

A proud gathering of 432nd TRW MiG killers with World War 2 fighter ace Gen John W Vogt Jr, then Seventh Air Force Command-in-Chief (second left, centre row), and Col Charles A Gabriel (third left, centre row). In the back line are, from left to right, Capts Larry Pettit and Fred Olmsted, Lt Col Jim Cooney and Capts Jim Null and Steve Eaves. In the centre row, from left to right, are Capt Keith Jones, Gen Vogt, Col Gabriel and Capts Jeff Feinstein and Steve Ritchie. Finally, in the front row are 1Lt John Markle and Maj Bart Crews (*via Lt Col K Jones*)

attack AAA positions en route. In a textbook operation, Roger Locher, by now 30 lbs lighter, was recovered without loss to the rescuers. The duration of his evasion in enemy territory and the distance that the force penetrated into North Vietnam for the rescue were both unprecedented.

WINNING WAYS

Another MiG-21 fell on 11 May, although its destroyers, Capt Stephen E Nichols and 1Lt James Bell, had to wait two years for confirmation of their kill. Their 555th TFS F-4D (66-7661) had already downed a MiG-17 on 14 February 1968. 'Gopher' flight, led by MiG killer Lt Col Joe Kittinger, was MiGCAPping a strike on bridges and airfields near Hanoi when two unidentified aircraft were sighted ahead. 'Gopher 1' set off in pursuit for a visual ID. When he had confirmed them as MiG-21s, Col Kittinger passed the lead to his wingman, Steve Nichols, for a shot.

Immediately after launching their missile, Nichols and Bell were horrified to see their leader's jet struck in the rear by a missile and burning. It crashed, taking its pilot and WSO (Bill Reich) into ten months of captivity. Nichols' kill remained unconfirmed, since the distraction of seeing his leader hit meant that he never saw his missile strike home. It was also implied that 'Gopher 1' had been hit by a stray AIM-7, but it was eventually proven that Nichols' missile was the only Sparrow launched that day, and that it did hit the MiG-21. 'Gopher 1' had been attacked by a third, trailing 927th FR MiG-21 flown by Ngo Van Phu (although VPAF records suggested that his was also the MiG destroyed by Nichols and Bell).

MiG engagements continued on 12 May, with the sixth consecutive kill for the 555th TFS. The squadron boss, Lt Col Wayne T Frye, with Lt Col James P Cooney, head of the 432nd TRW's operations tactics division, as his WSO, were the first F-4 crew with such high rank to down a MiG. They flew as number 2 in 'Harlow' F-4D MiGCAP flight north-west of Yen Bai. The lead pilot, Maj Sidney Hudson, saw a flight of four 925th FR MiG-19s leaving Yen Bai airfield. His WSO, Capt Larry H 'Doc' Pettit, takes up the story;

'We had lost our radar and had nothing but radar missiles. Sid had set up an orbit over a mountain just north-west of the field. As we were orbiting, Sid was getting lower and lower. Finally, Wayne Frye asked if Sid was doing what he thought he was doing. Sid said "Yup". Since we were near "bingo" fuel, he went really low over the Red River, accelerated to the speed of snot and popped up over the end of the Yen Bai airfield.

'Immediately in front of us were four MiG-19s on their take-off roll. We hit the speedboards and Sid asked me what mode the radar was in. I told him it was in boresight. He fired the first missile, although we were well inside any missile range. The MiGs' drop tanks went over our wings and I then saw a MiG in front of us. I could see the pilot twisting and turning in his seat to see what was going on. We were extremely close to the "gomer", and we fired the rest of our missiles while he continued to manoeuvre.

'We then turned south and were egressing when we observed the kill by Wayne "Fossil" Frye and Jim "Granny GIB" Cooney (with a combined age of 85, they were the most senior MiG killing team!). After we returned to the US, Sid called me and said we were asked to submit a claim for the

A pair of 4th TFS Phantom IIs wind up for take-off at Da Nang. Having transferred to the 35th TFS (LC codes) soon after this photograph was taken, 67-0281 (left) became the first F-4E MiG killer when Lt Col Lyle Beckers and Capt John Huwe claimed a MiG-19 destroyed during a 35th TFS chaff flight escort mission on 23 May 1972 (*via Peter Schinkelshoek*)

Capt James Beatty and 1Lt James Sumner flew F-4E-35-MC 67-0333 in 421st TFS/366th TFW LC codes for their 23 May 1972 MiG-21 kill. On that day the F-4E scored its first kills with a missile and with a gun in two engagements lasting only a couple of minutes in total (*Norm Taylor*)

manoeuvring MiG in front of us, since it had apparently crashed. We submitted it, but to no avail.'

Lt Col Frye had also maintained an altitude of 500 to 1000 ft as he pursued the four MiG-19s after Hudson and Pettit had downed the number three MiG. Wayne Frye recalled;

'I took on the number four MiG-19, and the rate of closure was quite high. I fired two AIM-4Ds – "heat seekers that didn't seek". Although I was at minimum range for arming, I then fired two AIM-7s and pulled sharply off the target, up and to the right, to avoid any missile or aircraft debris, only to find another MiG-19 filling my windscreen – an easy kill for an F-4E! Naturally, I had no time to investigate the results of my encounter with the first MiG, since we were at, or below, "bingo" fuel. Lead and I joined the second F-4D element for a return to base. After an airborne weapons check, and a "What luck?" from lead, I reported "one possible". Only after landing, and reports from the second element (who were 2-3 miles in trail) was the kill confirmed, and to this day I'm unsure since I didn't see it.'

Jim Cooney recalled that the Sparrows were fired first in boresight mode, then the AIM-4Ds, but agreed that, 'The AIM-4D was never famous for hitting anything! We were close-in, and I do mean very close!'

After these losses, the VPAF typically stayed out of the action for a while, but it responded on 18 May to a major USAF strike on fuel storage areas near Hanoi. One MiG-21 was damaged.

All the 1972 MiG kills up to that point had fallen to Udorn-based F-4Ds. On 23 May, the 35th TFS crews (detached from the 3rd TFW to

F-4E-35-MC 67-0333 is seen at Udorn with the 432nd TRW in the summer of 1973, the aircraft still proudly wearing its MiG kill on its nose from its 23 May 1972 engagement. Note that the jet also boasts the name *PRINCESS* on its gun housing. The Phantom II is carrying Mk 82 bombs under its wings and an ALQ-101 ECM pod in the left forward missile trough. Red 421st TFS marking around the canopy have been over-painted green, as has the sharks-mouth, acquired in 366th TFW service (*Col R Thurlow*)

the 366th TFW at Da Nang, and flying LC-coded aircraft) gave the F-4E variant its first two victories during a battle with eight MiGs.

Operating as 'Balter' flight, the F-4 crews were a chaff escort that switched to MiGCAP after the chaffers had finished their work. Lt Col Lyle C Beckers and Capt John Huwe had just led the flight past Kep airfield when they saw several silver MiGs circling the base, and others on approach. Beckers lined up on a pair of MiG-19s but the range closed too quickly and he momentarily lost sight of his target in the clouds. He had to overshoot, as his 'angle off' was too severe, and he repositioned for an approach at 550 knots and 1500 ft. The second MiG presented a good target against a clear sky background, and he was able to get a full-systems lock-on, ripple firing two AIM-7E-2s. The first ran straight into the MiG-19's fuselage and sent it downwards out of control.

The remaining five MiGs then set up a defensive 'wagon wheel' formation over their base, and Lyle Beckers tried repeatedly to break into it and pick off another target. Meanwhile, 'Balter 2' (Capt James Beatty and 1Lt James M Sumner) had covered their flight leader's attacks, and their watchful eyes picked up a pair of MiG-21s dashing in to attack the Americans. Capt Beatty swung into position behind one of them and selected 'guns', as he was too close for a missile shot. Letting his gunsight settle, he placed the 'pipper' one aircraft length ahead of the turning MiG

35th TFS (LC codes) and 4th TFS (LA codes) F-4Es of the 366th TFW share ramp space at Da Nang in early 1972. 67-0333 in the foreground is the MiG killer flown by Capt James Beatty and 1Lt James Sumner. The M61A-1 cannon was approved for the F-4E in October 1965 and tested in prototype RF-4C 62-12200 using an F-105-type installation, firing through the front camera window. Anti-shock mountings were crucial, as the gun's considerable vibration was generated just inches away from the aircraft's delicate avionics (*via Doug Malloy*)

and opened fire, using his tracer to aim the shells more effectively. At a range of 1000 yards he could see them chewing up the fighter, which began to disintegrate and soon rolled left and impacted the ground.

SPECKS THAT DON'T SMOKE

Two more MiG-21s were downed on 31 May, adding second kills for Capts Ritchie and Feinstein, albeit in separate engagements. Feinstein was WSO for Capt Bruce Leonard in F-4E 68-0338, flying as 'Gopher 3' . It was the second of two MiGCAP flights covering the strike force, but it was quickly drawn into action when MiGs were encountered near Kep. 'Gopher 3's' arduous encounter began when a MiG-21 was sighted at their 'ten o'clock', head on, as Bruce Leonard recalled;

'We went in as two four-ship MiGCAPs, and Ritchie's flight got into a fight first. Their fight went down to low altitude. We did a 180-degree turn, and as we were coming out, a beautiful-looking MiG appeared heading towards our "six o'clock", higher than we were. I could see him pulling his nose down, and I had to decide whether he was likely to pull his tail around and come after us. But then he just went away and we were then heading back out towards the Gulf. Our flight leader, John Lessenberg, being ever conscious of the "ground pounders" we were covering, called *Red Crown* to find out if they had all completed their mission and egressed the target. *Red Crown* said it would check, but John said, "Ah well, round we go again".

'We turned around for another orbit, and were heading back in, when John Bullock (lead WSO) sighted MiGs head-on. He couldn't get one because if you had to ID a MiG visually, head-on they appeared so small you were usually too close for a missile shot. If he'd had something like the TISEO (TV/telescopic sight) that we tested at Da Nang with the 389th TFS he might have sighted the MiGs 2000 ft earlier.

'We manoeuvred a little to the left, but one MiG was firing and closing in on me. He was turning left, so I took my element that way too, and as I rolled up on my left wing I saw a MiG at about 90 degrees off, going left, but too fast for me to do anything. Still, it looked like a real gift – a nice clear sky and all kinds of AIM-9E tone, so I fired one off on the basis of "fire for effect". We were pulling about 3-4g, so I never saw the missile, and he was turning too, so it never had a real chance. We rolled wings level and saw the lead F-4 element still going left, so I rolled up into another hard left turn, and there was another dull silver MiG sitting out there in front at about 90 degrees off. I thought that I would try and "pull with him". Later, when we listened to the cockpit tape, we could hear the cockpit g-warning beeper chirping away at this point!

'Then the guy made his mistake. He must have been following his element leader out ahead of him, and he suddenly rolled out of his turn, wings level, while he was still 40 degrees off my nose. If he'd kept going in his turn I wouldn't have got

Philco-Ford AIM-9J missiles and a 'two canister' ALQ-87 pod fill a pylon on this 'Triple Nickel' Phantom II. Initially called the AIM-9E Extended Performance missile under the *End Game 2* programme from 1968 to 1970, the AIM-9J had double the guidance duration of the AIM-9E, greater manoeuvrability via double-delta canard fins and improved guidance. Initial tests against drones produced a 92 per cent success rate. Improvements under the *Combat Snap* programme reduced the 'miss distance' from the target at missile detonation from the AIM-9E's 13.5 ft, but doubts remained about the warhead size, fusing and the hard-to-hear target acquisition 'buzz' tone (*Col R Thurlow*)

around for a shot at him. I kept pulling around to get in his direction, but by then he was just a dot, heading down towards cloud. I lowered the nose, put the pipper on that dot, got an AIM-9 missile tone and fired. At that moment Jeff Feinstein said, "We have two dots off to our left". We didn't know what they were, but they weren't smoking, so they were probably MiGs. Anyway, at that point lead said "Going feet wet", so we turned away without seeing the results of the AIM-9 shot and came back out with him. At debriefing we explained what had happened, but then we had to go on alert that night, so I couldn't have celebrated a kill in any case. Later, we had a report from intelligence sources that the MiG had crashed, so Third Air Force duly awarded us the kill.

'It was ironic that I was the one to get the MiG. At the mission briefing, we had been told "only the flight leader shoots". The rest of us were to concentrate on staying as a four-ship with our eyeballs out, covering the flight's backside. But John Lessenberg (who fired all four of his AIM-7s without a hit) was just throwing MiGs in front of me, and all I could do was try to shoot them!'

It was also another step on Jeff Feinstein's way to ace status, an honour that Bruce Leonard felt was well deserved;

'He was an excellent back-seater, always good at seeing threats and keeping the pilot informed, even turning around and kneeling on his seat to get better rearward visibility.'

Bruce Leonard saw five MiGs during his engagement, and there were others in the air. The other MiGCAP flight, 'Icebag', led by Steve Ritchie and 'Doc' Pettit, was taking on two 'blue' bandits that they had lured into the action by posing as a chaff flight. The MiG controllers intercepted their 'chaffer' call-signs and transmissions, despatching two MiG-21s to dispose of a seemingly easy target. *Red Crown* advised them of the MiGs' position at their 'eight o'clock', and Ritchie turned into them as they committed to an attack. Larry Pettit remembers;

'We did some turns, and I spotted two dots at our "seven o'clock" position. Steve turned hard, and had completed about 150 degrees when everyone spotted the bandits. We continued turning and wound up with the MiGs on our nose at "ten o'clock". I locked onto a MiG and Steve fired an AIM-7 that went haywire. At this time the lead MiG went straight up into the "menopause", leaving his unlucky number two to face the music. The second AIM-7 detonated early, as did the third. Steve called number 3 (John Madden) to be prepared to take over, and fired the fourth missile. It hit the MiG right behind the cockpit, cutting it in half. Both parts spiralled into oblivion. No 'chute was observed.'

John Madden as element leader ('Icebag 3') had his first experience of intense combat with MiGs during the engagement;

'We went up over the Gulf of Tonkin and came in over Cam Pha, north of Phantom Ridge. We had

Capts Terry Murphy, John Madden, Steve Ritchie and Maj Sam Newman pose for the camera. John Madden's 'party suit' carries his three MiG kill stars, and records his second-tour 100 missions over North Vietnam in F-4Cs with the 390th TFS out of Da Nang during *Rolling Thunder*. On that tour he flew mostly night missions, day-time route reconnaissance and some MiGCAPs. He then became an F-4 instructor at George AFB, where his students included a cadre of Israeli Air Force pilots. He attended a course at the Fighter Weapons School (he and Ritchie both have FWS patches on their suits) with pilots like Bob Lodge and Mike Ryan, who later became USAF Chief-of-Staff. John's third combat tour took him to Udorn, where he replaced Bob Lodge, who was approaching the end of his tour as 432nd TRW weapons and tactics officer. 'I had only been there a couple of days when Bob was shot down', he told the author (*Doug Hardgrave*)

36

slowed down to drop our centreline tanks – they had to be dropped "straight and level" at 300 knots. We were headed west, and they ran MiGs around in a left turn to get behind some bombers below us. One pilot saw he had overshot the target and climbed to 40,000 ft, getting out of the fight. The other MiG was 1.5 miles from us at our "11 o'clock", high in a 2g turn. I called to Steve Ritchie and he was able to pick him up and turn into him. As flight leader, Steve got him – his second kill.'

May 1972 had been a disastrous month for the VPAF, with 11 losses to USAF Phantom IIs and 16 to Navy F-4s. A major post-mortem commanders' conference was convened, and the resultant report called for revised tactics. Their losses would undoubtedly have been even higher if US missiles had not reached a low point in reliability.

The AIM-9E scored only 12 per cent of the kills during its first six months' use with the USAF, compared with 15 per cent for the earlier AIM-9B in *Rolling Thunder*. 'Dogfight' Sparrow became the weapon of choice in 1972, since it required less aircrew training in ACM than the Sidewinder, and could be fired head-on, at long range, or in relatively high-g turns. However, poor reliability reduced its effectiveness to less than 13 per cent – little better than the AIM-9E. Premature detonation or motor failure were frequent problems.

MILITANT MiGS

June 1972 brought a steady increase in MiG activity, causing the loss of seven USAF aircraft, all of them F-4s. Just two MiGs were shot down by USAF fighters in return (the US Navy claimed three more). A 432nd TRW MiGCAP flight pursued a decoy formation of MiG-19s on 13 June, but the F-4s were trapped from behind by two MiG-21s and F-4E 67-0365 (308th TFS) was hit. This loss cast further doubt over the 'fluid four' concept that often placed the number four jet in a vulnerable position and on this occasion sent two 1st lieutenants into captivity.

The MiGs' supersonic, slashing attacks from high behind the slower-moving F-4s were hard to handle. On the occasion of another 308th loss, flight leader Dan Miller reported that the 'MiG-21 came through so fast that pursuit was basically useless, but they tried anyway to no avail'.

WSO Capt Milt Katz is assisted by a 308th TFS crew chief as he deplanes from F-4E-35-MC 67-0337 at Udorn post mission (*Col Bill F McDonald*)

The Udorn Wing struck back on 21 June in a remarkable duel between a MiG-19 and a 58th TFS F-4E flown by Maj Phil Handley and 1Lt Jack Smallwood. Over 250 US aircraft were involved in attacks on the North's supply and transport network that day, and 'Hands' Handley's F-4E was leading 'Brenda' MiGCAP flight 40 miles north-east of Hanoi. The 58th TFS CO, John Downey, was element leader, with Bob Ellis on his wing.

In the event, the two elements became separated, partly due to a violent SAM break and then by the second element reaching 'bingo'

MiG killers Maj Phil Handley (right) and 1Lt John Smallwood pose with 308th TFS crew chief Sgt Steve Accup at Udorn after their MiG kill in Accup's F-4E 67-0210 on 2 June 1972. Bill McDonald remembered 2 June as an eventful day. 'I had just watched a "Jolly Green" helicopter coming over the field trailing green smoke and landing with Roger Locher aboard. Then, in the afternoon, F-4E '210 came over in formation with three other birds. Right over our revetments Handley cracked 'burner, pulling straight up and snap rolling twice. I was standing right underneath that victory roll - the first for a 308th TFS aircraft' (*Col Bill F McDonald*)

For 'Brenda' flight's MiG killing mission on 2 June 1972, Maj Phil Handley (in this jet) devised 'fluid two' tactics. 'I drew them out on the back of a napkin at the "O" Club the night before, briefed the flight next morning and they worked like a charm. I instructed "fluid four" for many years. When I flew the F-86 it was the way to go when altitude was king and you tried to get as high as possible. When you move the fight down into denser air at 15,000-20,000 ft, and turns are made with higher g-forces, the wingman doesn't have a chance during patrol turns. He simply becomes MiG bait' (*JEM via Col R Thurlow*)

fuel and egressing shortly thereafter. Maj Handley also began to take his element off CAP soon afterwards. He had jettisoned his 600-gallon 'bath-tub' fuel tank before coasting in to the target area, punching off his 370-gallon wing-tanks when they ran dry just before egress. His Homestead AFB Phantom II carried two AIM-7s in the rear wells, a pair of AIM-4s ('Hughes' Arrow in the Heart') outboard and an ALQ-87 pod in the forward left missile bay.

However, it was the M61 cannon that Phil Handley used to despatch one of a pair of MiG-19s that rose to intercept them as they left the CAP area. Warned in advance of the MiGs, he had accelerated. 'I wanted to get to "corner, plus a little" as soon as I knew that bandits were in the area'.

By the time he engaged the enemy he was at Mach 1.2, descending to 500 ft above the ground. The MiGs flew at 90 degrees across the F-4s' flight path, travelling at 500 knots. At a slant range of only 200-300 ft, Handley triggered his cannon and the second MiG was hit. As he pulled his F-4E (67-0210) up into a vertical climb, Handley and his wingman crew (Capts Stan Green and Douglas Eden) saw the MiG streaming fire and losing altitude, with its wings rocking alarmingly. Seconds later it flopped to the ground and exploded in a burgeoning fireball.

On his return to Udorn, Maj Handley discovered that his incredibly accurate snap shot had used virtually all his ammunition;

'I was supposed to have a full load of 20 mm, but someone had fired the gun on a previous sortie, failed to note it on the form and left only 310 rounds aboard out of 640. This was discovered in post-flight inspection when an armourer found only ten rounds remaining after I had fired my three-second burst.'

Realising the effectiveness of the USAF's air-dropped chaff 'corridors' in disrupting their air defence control, the North Vietnamese had begun concentrated attacks on F-4 'chaffers', and their escorts. Flying in-line abreast, with up to eight aircraft behind the *Iron Hand* flights, the Phantom IIs dropped their M-129 chaff bombs at about 20-second intervals, creating a corridor up to six miles wide and over 30 miles in length that protected the strike force throughout the SAM threat area. Flying at low speed, set altitude and straight-and-level, the 'chaffers' were tempting targets. The mission was often assigned to TDY 'summer help' units like the Seymour-Johnson based 4th TFW detachments. It was risky for the escort flights too. Nine of the eighteen F-4 losses during *Linebacker I* were 'chaffers' or chaff escorts.

Lt Col Von R Christiansen and Maj Kaye M Harden (469th TFS) were element leaders in 'Iceman' flight, escorting two flights of chaff bombers on 21 June 1972.

Three MiG-21s flew across their path unexpectedly and one attacked the 'chaffers', downing a 334th TFS F-4E (69-0282) which had not heard the warning call. The other two MiGs turned towards the F-4 escorts and fired two 'Atolls' at the leader, Col Mele Vojvodich and his wingman. Both were evaded when 'Iceman 3' called a warning.

The two MiGs apparently failed to see Christiansen and his wingman because they continued flying straight, with afterburners blazing.

Christiansen accelerated his element at full power to a position 5000 ft behind the MiGs, while Maj Harden got a full-systems lock-on and tried to launch a pair of AIM-7s. Neither missile left the aircraft. With the MiGs in range for an IR missile, the pilot ripple-fired three AIM-9Es. The first exploded 50 ft to the MiG's right as he made a shallow dive. Harden observed the second Sidewinder hit the MiG's tail, causing an immediate fireball and forcing the pilot to take to his yellow 'chute.

Meanwhile, Lt Col Christiansen pulled up in afterburner to pursue a MiG-21 that was threatening both 'Iceman 1' and '2'. A violent, turning engagement took him from 20,000 ft down to 1000 ft. With his missiles spent, he fired short bursts of 20 mm, scoring a few hits on the MiG, before reaching 'bingo' fuel. 'Iceman 4', with a complete load of missiles and 20 mm, followed his element leader without getting a firing opportunity. Christiansen's was the first confirmed 388th TFW kill since 23 August 1967, at which point the unit was still flying F-105Ds.

It was over two weeks before the next MiG kill, but eight USAF F-4s were lost to MiGs during that time. Two were from the 366th TFW on their first day of operations from Takhli RTAFB after moving from Da Nang. The VPAF had recently introduced the MiG-21J, and its fighter regiments also benefited from much-improved GCI systems.

The equilibrium was partly restored on 8 July when three MiGs were destroyed. Capts Richard 'Tuna' Hardy and Paul Lewinski (4th TFS) downed the first during another chaff escort. 'Brenda' flight shepherded

469th TFS 'bomb truck' F-4Es 67-0315 and 67-0385 take it in turns to suckle from their 'life-support system' en route to North Vietnam. Both aircraft carry single AIM-7s in their rear missile wells – useful if attacked by a MiG, although other ordnance would have been jettisoned first to allow them to be fired (*via C W Moggeridge*)

Lt Col Von Christiansen and Maj Kaye Harden's MiG-killing F-4E (67-0283) is seen at Korat RTAFB in May 1974 displaying its victory star, repainted sharksmouth and 34th TFS codes. It has also been retrofitted with the longer, stainless steel Midas IV gun fairing that was installed on F-4Es in the factory from Block 48 onwards, and retrospectively on earlier examples. Louvres below the gun housing expelled gun gas downwards, and a T-4 de-enrichment device allowed any ingested gas to bypass the engines (*Centurion Enterprises via Alan Howarth*)

the 'chaffers' safely out of danger and then returned for a sweep operation. As they headed out again, MiGs attempted to catch them from the rear – a familiar tactic based on the assumption that F-4 crews would be short of fuel and relaxing their guard for the homeward trip. 'Brenda' lead attempted to attack the first MiG, but the F-4E (69-7563) was damaged by an 'Atoll'. Lt Col Ross and his WSO, Capt Stan Imaye (who was to score a MiG-21 with Lt Col Gene Taft later in that month), ejected over Thailand and were recovered.

Meanwhile, the second MiG-21 overshot 'Brenda' flight, giving Capts Hardy and Lewinski a good firing opportunity. They launched an AIM-9E that failed to guide, and then attempted to ripple-fire their other three Sidewinders. All of them stubbornly remained on their launch rails, so the crew set up a boresight launch for a pair of AIM-7E-2s. The first scored a direct hit, blowing off the MiG's right wing. Their second missile impacted the wreck, compounding its destruction.

The other two MiGs destroyed that day fell to Capts Steve Ritchie and Chuck DeBellevue. Flying as lead for 'Paula' flight in F-4E 67-0362, they were covering the departure of a strike force when MiGs were vectored towards them. *Disco* and *Red Crown* warned 'Paula 1' that MiGs were actually threatening the *Disco* EC-121 radar picket as it circled at low altitude only a few miles from them. Turning towards the enemy, Ritchie saw a MiG pass overhead, but kept the flight on its northerly heading until he saw a second, trailing MiG behind its leader, turning in order to

This 4th TFS/366th TFW F-4E-33-MC (66-0340) remained at Phu Cat AB, in South Vietnam, for 30 days in order that repairs could be carried out to its right wing root which had been damaged by a 50-calibre flak shell during a mission 'up North'. A number of early F-4Es arrived in South-east Asia with black-and-tan radomes (*Norm Taylor*)

A 58th TFS patch, TAC shield and blue fin cap decorate 67-0362, which was the F-4E in which Capts Steve Ritchie and Chuck DeBellevue destroyed two MiG-21s on 8 July 1972. Improvements to the E-model Phantom II culminated in the production of the *Rivet Haste* slatted F-4E. In triple MiG killer John Madden's opinion, 'the USAF finally got an F-4 that we were pretty satisfied with. It led to the F-15 that the Air Force designed from the ground up' (*Norm Taylor via Alan Howarth*)

trap the F-4s. He pulled hard left and reached a position low in the second MiG's 'five o'clock'. There, the crew set up a boresight launch and fired a pair of Sparrows. The MiG pilot noticed his adversary seconds too late and the first missile turned his fighter into an inferno as he made a belated attempt to evade it.

Ritchie had maintained his flight's four-ship integrity, and he 'unloaded' to gain energy, taking 'Paula' into a hard right turn to engage the lead MiG as it returned to threaten 'Paula 4'. With their F-4 in a 5g turn below the MiG's 'five o'clock' position, Ritchie and DeBellevue launched another AIM-7 at the very edges of the missile's envelope. They immediately prepared for a follow-up gun attack, since they did not expect the missile to guide under such high g forces. In fact, it made the necessary sharp right turn and guided perfectly into its target, blowing the MiG-21 apart. It was DeBellevue's third MiG and the fourth for Ritchie. The pressure was on to enable him to become the first USAF F-4 ace.

MULTI-MISSION PHANTOM IIs

With the addition of chaff flights and their escorts, plus LGB bombing, the demands on the F-4 wings increased. Within the increasingly 'all F-4' tactical force, the squadrons specialised. Ubon had the dedicated day squadrons (the 25th and 433rd TFSs, the latter having also pioneered LGB delivery) and two concentrating on night operations (the 435th and 497th TFSs). On its transfer from Ubon to Udorn in June 1968, the 555th TFS had retained its F-4Ds and its primary air-to-air mission. Ubon also took over some chaff missions, and the bulk of the MiGCAP work went to Udorn and the Korat-based F-4 units, some of which were assigned on a TDY basis.

However, within this mighty F-4 community there was an ever-diminishing number of crews with substantial air-to-air experience or training. Few of the *Rolling Thunder* veterans remained, and the flow of rapidly trained replacement aircrews often received their only air-to-air training when they arrived in-theatre. Consequently, the number of crews qualified to fly MiGCAPs was quite small, and in many cases they were veteran pilots who had been persuaded back for second tours.

This also caused problems for squadron schedulers like Col Cooper, who had to avoid overworking the expert crews, while at the same time ensuring that no MiGCAP went out on patrol with an inadequate level of expertise in the flight. As Bruce Leonard observed, relying on a succession

Basking in a Korat revetment, this 34th TFS F-4E-35-MC displays some interesting variations on the standard camouflage scheme. Post-war, 67-0315's crash on take-off on 5 September 1986 ended a period of 115,890.2 flight hours without mishap for its owners at that time, the 335th TFS/4th TFW – the longest-ever fighter safety record (*via Michael France*)

of crews who 'visited' the war for relatively short tours or TDYs was a 'funny way to run a war'.

The VPAF had no such problems since many of its surviving pilots (like those in the Luftwaffe in World War 2) flew throughout the war, gaining experience and expertise all the time.

Among the longest-serving and most experienced USAF units in the war was the 13th TFS 'Black Panthers' (or 'Panther Pack'), assigned to the 432nd TRW in October 1967. The next MiG kill fell to the unit on 18 July when WSO Capt Jeff Feinstein got his third MiG-21. His 'nose gunner' was Lt Col Carl Baily, flying *Combat Tree* F-4D 66-0271 as 'Snug 1'. Inexperience probably caused 'Snug 4' to make a hard turn to the right as soon as he sighted bandits, and this broke up the flight. Baily elected to press on with his wingman since MiGs were harassing another F-4 flight that was approaching 'bingo' fuel.

Three minutes later Feinstein established a *Combat Tree* contact and guided the element towards it until Baily could see a single silver MiG-21. With a full-systems lock-on, all four of their AIM-7E-2s were fired as the MiG dived steeply to escape, causing all four to miss. Baily quickly followed up with an AIM-9E that found its mark, blowing off the MiG's right wing at low altitude and making the jet snap-roll into the ground. Its pilot ejected but he landed in a tree – he later died of his injuries.

The same team racked up another victory on 29 July in 'Cadillac' MiGCAP, orbiting near Kep airfield to cover a strike on the north-east railway. Two MiG-21s slipped through and Nguyen Tien Sam shot down one of the 'chaffers' (F-4E 66-0367 of the 4th TFS) by using the high-Mach slashing attack and withdrawal tactic that the MiG units had re-introduced that month. *Red Crown* vectored 'Cadillac' towards the VPAF jets, and Baily and Feinstein's F-4D (66-0271 again) acquired *Combat Tree* indications, then a radar lock-on to a pair of MiGs over ten minutes later. They entered a turning fight in which the lead MiG-21 consistently kept out of range, breaking their radar lock at six miles.

They soon re-acquired it, and another 'Cadillac' F-4 (1Lt Kirchner and Capt Rogers) saw a silver MiG-21 ahead. *Red Crown* advised them that two more bandits were also out ahead. Lt Col Baily, as 'shooter', launched three AIM-7E-2s. The first suffered ignition failure, but the other two exploded near the VPAF fighter, which immediately burst into flames.

Capt Stan Imaye's kill happened on the same morning when he flew as WSO in 'Pistol 1' for a chaff escort flight. Under serious threat from SAMs and MiGs, the chaff flights pulled out, leaving their two escort flights to tangle with the MiG-21s. 'Pistol' flight was immediately attacked, and the lead Phantom II's pilot, Lt Col Gene Taft, managed to get behind one of them. After initial difficulty in acquiring a lock-on, he was able to lock the MiG in boresight mode when it levelled out at a range of 9000 ft. Lt Col Taft counted to four and squeezed the trigger. His AIM-7 flew straight and true, starting an inferno in the MiG's wing area. It lurched into an uncontrollable roll, but 'Pistol' flight had to turn away before seeing it impact the ground. Instead, they saw F-4E 66-0367 crashing in flames as they departed, its crew ejecting into captivity.

As July 1972 closed, so did the USAF's unfavourable kill-to-loss ratio against the VPAF. From August to the end of *Linebacker*, four MiGs were destroyed for every F-4 or F-105G casualty.

ACE MAKING

August 1972 brought four more kills, with the first of them being claimed by an exchange crew. Capt Larry Richard (US Marine Corps) and Lt Cdr Mike Ettel (US Navy) (see *Osprey Combat Aircraft 30 - US Navy F-4 Phantom II MiG Killers* for details) were flying with the 58th TFS on a weather reconnaissance south-east of Yen Bai when they were warned of bandits commencing an attack from 30 miles away. The three F-4Es and one RF-4C of Capt Richard's 'Dodge' flight divided into two elements, with one at higher altitude to cover 'Dodge 1' as Richard steered left after two MiG-21s that he had sighted.

Slowing, and jettisoning their wing tanks with a brief 'positive g' manoeuvre, 'Dodge 1' and '2' slipped in behind the MiGs unseen, and Larry Richard got a boresight lock-on to the silver, leading jet at a range of two miles. Closing to around 1300 ft, he launched an AIM-7E-2. Seconds before impact, the MiG pilot caught sight of the Sparrow's long white 'tail' of smoke and broke hard towards 'Dodge 1', passing canopy to canopy. Richard and Ettel responded by 'unloading' their F-4E (67-0239) of g and locking on the second MiG – a light green, camouflaged example. Its pilot apparently had not realised that his leader had dived away and run for home. Richard fired a second AIM-7 at a distance of one mile and it blew the MiG's tail off.

Throughout the engagement Richard's wingman crew in their RF-4C clung to their position as enforced onlookers in the combat, but the pilot insisted on painting a half-MiG kill star on his unarmed RF-4C after the mission. Richard and Ettel's genuine kill was confirmed by the crew of 'Dodge 3', Lt Col Lee Williams and Maj Tom Leach.

Capt Bryan Tibbett (left) and 1Lt William 'Bud' Hargrove talk tactics with US Navy exchange pilot Lt Cdr Mike Ettel (US Navy) in September 1972 at Udorn RTAFB. With Capt Larry Richard (US Marine Corps exchange pilot) in the front seat of his Phantom II, Mike Ettel downed a MiG-21 on 12 August 1972 (*USAF via Col R Thurlow*)

FLYING 'CHAFF'

The beleaguered chaff flights had a chance to show their teeth on 15 August when 'Date' flight came under attack by a MiG-21. Aircraft number 4 in the flight (F-4E 69-7235) was flown by Capts Fred Sheffler and Mark Massen in an eight-aircraft formation consisting entirely of 336th TFS 'Rocketeers' F-4Es. Sheffler recalled;

'When we got to Ubon the 8th TFW wanted to split our guys and aeroplanes up among the other squadrons there. We had F-4Es and they had F-4Ds. When this reached the ears of our former wing commander, Brig Gen Cotton Hildreth, he raised the roof and said "No!" We kept our unit intact. I suspect that out of retribution we got the dregs of the missions flown from Ubon for a long time. Our motto soon became "Dumb Bombs, Smart Bombers", as we got most of the close air support and almost all the "dumb" (as opposed to LGB) bombing missions.

'One very undesirable mission that fell to the 336th TFS was dropping chaff. On those occasions we then called ourselves the "Chaffeteers" (rather than "Rocketeers"). The new AN/ALE-38 chaff pod had recently been deployed, and it was used first at Udorn. One of their troops had accidentally jettisoned one over Laos, so the mission was transferred to Ubon (and the ejection cartridges removed from the pylons that carried the pods). We flew as an eight-ship, line-abreast formation. Each F-4 had one ALE-38, four chaff bombs on the centreline to provide vertical protection from SAMs and an ECM pod in the left, forward missile well. We replaced the Wild Weasels in being the first jets on target.'

The squadron was assured that the chaff cloud would protect the 'chaffers' as well as the bombers. On one occasion Fred counted 70 SA-2s climbing through the Phantom II flight, but exploding only as they exited the chaff cloud above the F-4s. On 15 August the chaff flight was tasked with covering two targets – the Viet Tri thermal power plant and a railway bridge at Phu Tho, which was attacked by two LGB-toting strike forces on different ingress routes. 'Date' flight, led by squadron CO Lt Col D C Vest, and 'Palm' flight, headed by Capt Rudy V Zuberbuhler, fought through a line of thunderstorms to reach the target area.

As the squadron's standardisation and evaluation (stan-eval) officer, Fred Sheffler had put another pilot, Tim Libertore, in the 'Date 2' slot for a tactical check ride. This placed Sheffler's F-4E as 'Blue 4' on the extreme right of the eight-ship phalanx – ideally placed for a close-up view of the MiG-21 that suddenly passed by 200 ft off his right wing. Warning was minimal. The usual intelligence agencies such as *Red Crown* and *Teaball* were 'down' that day, and the first warning came from 'Pistol' flight (a two-ship chaff escort from Da Nang) seconds before the bandit appeared.

'To our surprise', Fred recalled, 'it was camouflaged overall medium green, with a white centreline tank. The pilot had a white helmet'. It was one of the first camouflaged MiG-21s to be sighted. 'Had "Pistol" flight not spotted the MiGs I might have ended up in the "Hanoi Hilton", or worse. He sped by at Mach 1.1, not turning, while we were at 0.95 Mach'.

The mission tape from 'Date 4' recorded 'Pistol' calling, 'Take it to the right, Date!' as the MiG overshot. Seconds later Capt Harv Smith, element leader in 'Date 3' called, 'Take the lead, Fred, take the lead!'

Several MiG-killer F-4Ds from *Rolling Thunder* returned to Southeast Asia for *Linebacker* duties. One such aircraft was F-4D 66-7594, seen here in 435th TFS/8th TFW markings soon after it was used to down a MiG-17 by Lt Col Squier and 1Lt Muldoon on 3 January 1968. The jet later saw much action in 1972 with the 388th TFW at Korat RTAFB, wearing JJ codes (*Norm Taylor*)

As Fred Sheffler reflected;

'I was lucky enough to survive, and get quick vengeance, but really that luck was due to a lot of training in snap lock-ons with the "556 radar mod" that our squadron had practised during air intercept training back at Seymour-Johnson. It was second nature to go for the auto-lock as the MiG spit out in front of me.'

The same cockpit tape revealed Massen and Sheffler selecting radar auto-acquisition at that exact moment. Only 1.5 seconds after the call to 'take the lead', an AIM-7E-2 was launched from 'Date 4', and 11 seconds after that the intruding MiG was hit squarely in its wing-root just as its pilot began a hard break to the left;

'There was a very large fireball that was still burning on the ground 15 minutes later as the strike force F-4s departed. No 'chute was observed. When I fired, the MiG was at about "11 o'clock" on my windscreen, and the AIM-7 took off in a "10 o'clock" direction. For a second I thought it was not guiding, but it had already figured out the crossing angle of the target and was just taking the shortest course. Others in the flight said the missile only made a slight correction at the last moment. Those 11 seconds of flight put the AIM-7 at the furthest extreme of its capability, for the motor burned out after about three seconds. When I locked onto the MiG, its opening velocity (acceleration away from the F-4E) was 300 knots at around 10,000 ft.'

Capts Sheffler and Massen quickly redirected their attention to the MiG's wingman as he made a hard left turn between the two F-4 flights;

'Date 3 and I continued in a spiral for several turns as we checked for the second MiG, and then we egressed. As we did so, I saw a silver jet coming in the opposite direction. Location, timing and direction matched the expected ingress of the F-105Gs, but I figured that it was a MiG. Neither of us turned to engage. Given our fuel state, I chose to egress rather than attempt a tail-chase. He was probably low on fuel too.'

Vietnamese records list two MiG-21s lost that day from a section led by seven-kill ace Dang Ngoc Ngu. They had been held on patrol over Hung Yen due to a similar GCI fault that had rendered the Americans' 'blind' that day, leaving them short of fuel by the time they ran into the 336th TFS F-4Es over Hoa Binh. The second MiG seen by Capt Sheffler's crew was vectored back to Phuc Yen by GCI, but was then diverted to Kep, where US intelligence later assessed that it ran out of fuel and crashed, accounting for the second pilot loss that the VPAF admitted to that day.

Fred Sheffler was able to paint a star on his F-4E's intake on his return to Thailand. It recorded the last MiG kill by a Ubon-based aircraft, and the only one for the 4th TFW detachments. 'The MiG kill meant a lot to the 336th', Fred asserted. 'Flying the chaff mission was a thankless job. If you can imagine having a grandstand seat to a MiG kill, and seeing it splashed right in front of you, you can understand my squadronmates' elation'. The eight-ship line-up of 'chaffers' watching the event consisted entirely of 336th TFS crews and aircraft.

The communications problems that almost allowed the MiG force to pick off 'Date 4' came at a time when the various intelligence and GCI agencies were attempting to channel all relevant information through a single location. Known as *Teaball*, this intel centre was established at Nakhon Phanom RTAFB at the end of July 1972. It coordinated

MiG killer Fred Sheffler took this self-portrait while on the look out for 'bandits' from the front cockpit of his F-4E in the summer of 1972 (*Fred Sheffler*)

information on the MiG threat from *Red Crown* radar ships, *Disco* EC-121Ts and a whole range of more covert sources, including the monitoring of North Vietnamese radio and IFF sources. However, the system had many teething problems throughout the summer of 1972, sometimes leaving aircrews in doubt about which agency, if any, would provide the warnings and guidance they required. These problems were compounded by the unreliable radio equipment specified for the F-4 and other tactical aircraft.

As further proof of the value of chaff escort flights, the next MiG kill was by a 'Pistol' flight aircraft on 19 August. Capt Sam White was flying his 204th, and penultimate, combat mission. With Capt Frank Bettine, he led the second element of a four-ship 'chaff CAP'. His 4th TFS F-4E (69-0291), loaded with four AIM-9Es, a pair of AIM-7E-2s and ECM pods in both forward missile wells, plus three external fuel tanks, took off from Takhli RTAFB – home of the 366th TFW following its arrival from Da Nang in early July 1972.

Taking up a position behind the chaff flights, the F-4Es flew a 'weaving' formation so as to protect them from attack from the rear by hard-to-spot MiG-21s. While the *Iron Hand* F-105Gs neutralised nearby SAM sites, a 'MiGs airborne' warning came from *Red Crown*. A single Phuc Yen-based MiG-21 had approached the formation over Hanoi at very low altitude, climbing to a position 3500 ft behind 'Pistol' flight.

'Pistol 2's WSO, Capt Forrest Penney, was the first to see the bandit boring in on them. 'Pistol 1' and '2' broke hard left, and Capt White engaged afterburner, climbing and rolling over the MiG's flightpath. The VPAF pilot, realising that he was no longer in a position to attack either element, dived away. White's barrel roll placed him below and behind the MiG, going supersonic. Both pilots performed roll manoeuvres, and the MiG pilot losing sight of his adversary in his blind spot.

Capts White and Bettine set up radar auto-acquisition, getting a full systems lock-on and firing both AIM-7E-2s. The missiles hit the enemy

'Triple Nickel' MiG shooters enjoy a drink at the Udorn 'O' Club in July 1972. They are, in the back row, from left to right, Lt Cols Wayne Frye and Jim Cooney, Capt Larry Pettit and 1Lt John Markle. In the front row, from left to right, are Capts Doug Hardgrave, Chuck DeBellevue, Steve Ritchie and Roger Locher (*via Doug Hardgrave*)

F-4E-34-MC 67-0278 features the orange/yellow trim of the 4th TFS. Assigned to the 366th TFW on 12 April 1969, the unit was issued with LA codes at the same time. It kept them when it moved to Takhli RTAFB on 27 June 1972, and again on assignment to the 432nd TRW at Udorn RTAFB on 31 October 1972. In August 1973 the squadron finally switched to UD codes in line with the rest of the 432nd TFW (*via Alan Howarth*)

fighter in quick succession. Its pilot bailed out and the wreckage crashed onto the mountains known as MiG Ridge. The victorious 'Pistol' crew immediately began to search for the MiG's wingman, but he had become separated earlier and was chased back to the sanctuary of Gia Lam Airport, Hanoi, by another F-4 MiGCAP. Capt White's element had by then reached 'bingo' fuel, so they headed for a tanker, then Takhli, a victory roll and a post-kill ceremonial hose-down by a fire-truck crew.

ACE RACE

It took seven years of aerial combat in Vietnam to produce the first USAF ace, which was a reflection on the comparative rarity of MiG encounters. By mid-1972 there were only two eligible flyers in the running for that honour – Capts Jeff Feinstein and Steve Ritchie. Both scored their fourth MiGs in July 1972, having had claims disallowed following June engagements. By this stage many Udorn crews felt that the Air Force was desperate to make an ace, and stories abounded to the effect that Steve Ritchie's chances were being enhanced by putting him in the best maintained jets with the latest equipment and weapons on board.

The matter was settled on 28 August when a *Linebacker* MiGCAP led by Ritchie and Capt Chuck DeBellevue met MiGs. *Disco* had taken control of MiG warnings that day after another *Teaball* glitch, and the three MiGCAP flights were vectored onto two MiG-21s as they egressed the target area. With 12 F-4s heading for the bandits, Ritchie recalled earlier advice that the MiG-21s had reverted to high altitude patrols.

Searching the sky above them, Ritchie and DeBellevue saw the MiGs at around 30,000 ft, approaching head on. They made a steep, climbing turn to a position behind the MiGs and fired two AIM-7E-2s at extreme range, hoping that these missiles would force the enemy to turn and engage. As the F-4D flight rolled out at altitude into a stern chase, Ritchie fired his other two Sparrows. Although the third missed its mark, the fourth AIM-7 struck a MiG-21 squarely. Element leader Capt Madden saw the jet tumble in flames.

On returning to base, the first man to climb the crew ladder and congratulate Ritchie on his fifth kill, and 'acedom', was crew chief Sgt Reggie Taylor. The number four MiG kill star on the flank of 'his' F-4D was Ritchie's first, from 10 May 1972. Taylor quickly added another red star to the scoreboard of the indomitable F-4D 66-7463. For good measure, he added a 'smiley face' sticker to the star's centre.

KILLER SHARKS

Korat RTAFB's sharkmouthed F-4Es were next to rack up a MiG after a long gap since their first victory on 21 June 1972. Maj Jon Lucas (34th TFS) and 1Lt Doug Malloy were element leaders in a 2 September hunter-killer *Iron Hand*

Lt Col Carl Baily (right), commander of the 13th TFS, and Capt Jeff Feinstein (centre) had to eject from their *Combat Tree* F-4D (66-7482) when it was hit by 37 mm AAA at 3000 ft near Haiphong on 25 August 1972. A 37th ARRS HH-53 'Jolly Green' rescue helicopter plucked them from the Tonkin Gulf, and they were still dripping when 432nd TRW commander, Col Scott G Smith (left), welcomed them back to Udorn with a sustaining beverage (*USAF via Col R Thurlow*)

Looking fairly anonymous, F-4D-29-MC 66-7463 is seen prior to its MiG killing days. On delivery to Udorn on 4 January 1972, it retained the UP codes of its former unit, the 35th TFS, before adopting 555th TFS OY codes (*via Michael France*)

Seen a decade later, 66-7463 displays its 'six shooter' scoreboard while serving with the 309th TFS/31st TTW at Homestead AFB, in Florida, in February 1982 (*Norm Taylor*)

flight comprising two CBU and bomb-armed F-4Es and a pair of F-105G Wild Weasels to detect and mark the SAM site with missiles.

Operating as 'Eagle' flight lead, Lucas and Malloy flew close by Phuc Yen airfield, and 20+ SAMs were launched at them as they 'worked' the target. Malloy recalled, 'We had attacked a SAM site while the F-105s covered us, and we were coming off target when a MiG-19 appeared in front of us. He had arrived from the direction of Hanoi, and was firing "Atoll" missiles at the "Thuds"'.

One of them was streaking towards F-105G 'Eagle 1', flown by Majs Tom Coady and Harold Kurtz, but they avoided the missile by making the hardest turn their jet could manage. The light blue MiG-19 then fired at 'Eagle 2', but Maj Cleveland and Captain O'Brien yanked their F-105G away from its cannon fire. As the VPAF pilot turned above Lucas and Malloy's 'Eagle 3', Lucas made a hard left turn to follow him, calling Doug to use auto-acquisition. They got a good lock-on, and Malloy counted the mandatory four seconds before pulling the trigger;

'We launched the left, aft AIM-7E-2 at the MiG, but at the same time an SA-2 started to track us. We evaded the SAM and started to egress from the target area, passing about 200 ft from a guy under a parachute. Our Sparrow had impacted the MiG while we were

Maj Jon Lucas (34th TFS) and WSO 1Lt Doug Malloy climb out of F-4E 67-0392 upon their return to Korat RTAFB after downing a MiG-19 on 2 September. They were element leaders in a hunter-killer flight, which was a relatively new concept for F-4E crews as Doug Malloy explained. 'Maj Lucas was the "Tiger" FAC commander at Korat, having been given the responsibility of reviving the hunter-killer mission in South-east Asia. On this mission he was training me, in his back seat, and my usual aircraft commander, Jim Kiloran, was piloting "Eagle 4" in our formation. I was a member of the 35th TFS/3rd TFW, on TDY from Kunsan AB, in Korea. We considered ourselves "summer help", but the 35th TFS did exceptionally well because we had many very experienced aircraft commanders, a number of them Fighter Weapons School graduates. Most of the WSOs were like me though, fresh out of RTU. Anyway, we accounted for six MiGs in the air and eight more on the ground' (*via Doug Malloy*)

doing our SAM break, and the F-105 crews had watched the show.'

Among the latter was Maj Cleveland, who saw the burning MiG-19 spiralling to earth.

The heavy *Linebacker* strikes on 9 September yielded three more victories, one of which put Chuck DeBellevue one MiG ahead of Steve Ritchie as leading USAF ace. All three MiGs fell to the 555th TFS MiGCAP orbiting near Phuc Yen. The flight leader was Capt John A. Madden, with Capt Charles DeBellevue as WSO.

John Madden's long preparation for his double MiG kill that day had

been thorough, and it illustrates the wealth of experience that some F-4 aircrew brought to the challenges of *Linebacker*. He graduated from flight school in 1964 in a class from which he was one of only four students who drew assignments in the then-new F-4C;

'At that stage they put pilots in the back seat as well as the front, since the leadership figured that two pilots would be a good thing. It didn't work very well, as it frustrated the pilots. I spent two years in the back seat with experienced pilots – a good education. Early on, I got selected for a joint Air Force/Navy test team that explored the AIM-7's capabilities in a manoeuvring environment. Firing the missiles at manoeuvring drones, I got very familiar with the AIM-7.'

His first combat tour was with the 43rd TFS's 'D' flight, augmenting the 431st TFS at Ubon, followed by a period at Cam Ranh Bay in 1966.

'I flew up to North Vietnam often, but the nearest I got to a MiG was a lock-onto one that followed us out of the North but then turned back.'

Returning to the USA, Madden was checked out as a front-seater and returned for a second tour, this time with the 390th TFS at Da Nang. His experience over North Vietnam taught him an abiding respect for many of the VPAF's pilots;

'They were formidable opponents – smart and absolutely respected. They used an awful lot of ruses and deceptions. It was clear that they were very disciplined and trained, thinking things through carefully. They loved to set traps and sucker people into them. It was just through the sheer numbers of aircraft we put up that we were able to overpower them.

'Some pilots were obviously better than others. You could tell after the first turn or two whether the pilot was really good or just learning. They would try a tactic and grow bolder with it until they took a hit. If they lost somebody they absolutely would not fly the next day. Then, over the next few days, they would start using other tactics in a measured way.'

This pragmatic approach often contrasted with the more rigid and predictable tactics used by American squadrons.

Madden and DeBellevue claimed two MiG-19s on 9 September, this type being encountered less often than the MiG-21, but far more frequently than the obsolescent MiG-17 (*text continues on page 62*).

Future MiG killer Lt Col Jim Brunson (second left) is seen here at a change of command ceremony in which he assumed control of the 555th TFS in the summer of 1972. *Rolling Thunder* MiG killer Capt Doug Hardgrave (left) organised and led the command change (*via Doug Hardgrave*)

Posing beneath the 432nd TRW's proud 'mission statement' at Udorn, Capts Jeff Feinstein (left) and John Madden are seen with US Navy Operations Specialist Chief Gene P Barnes. Serving aboard the guided missile cruiser USS *Truxton* (CGN-35), Barnes acted as a *Red Crown* controller for this F-4 crew's MiG kills (*USAF via Col R Thurlow*)

COLOUR PLATES

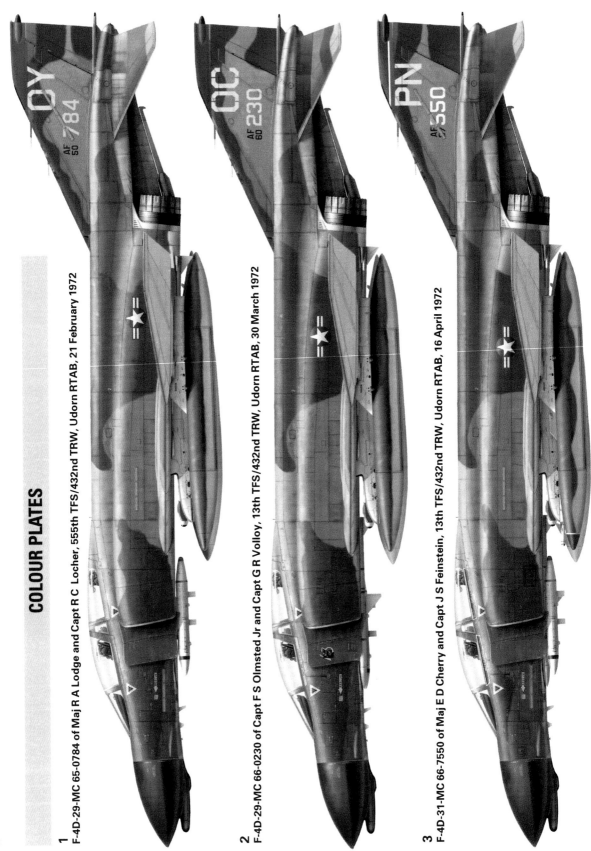

1
F-4D-29-MC 65-0784 of Maj R A Lodge and Capt R C Locher, 555th TFS/432nd TRW, Udorn RTAB, 21 February 1972

2
F-4D-29-MC 66-0230 of Capt F S Olmsted Jr and Capt G R Volloy, 13th TFS/432nd TRW, Udorn RTAB, 30 March 1972

3
F-4D-31-MC 66-7550 of Maj E D Cherry and Capt J S Feinstein, 13th TFS/432nd TRW, Udorn RTAB, 16 April 1972

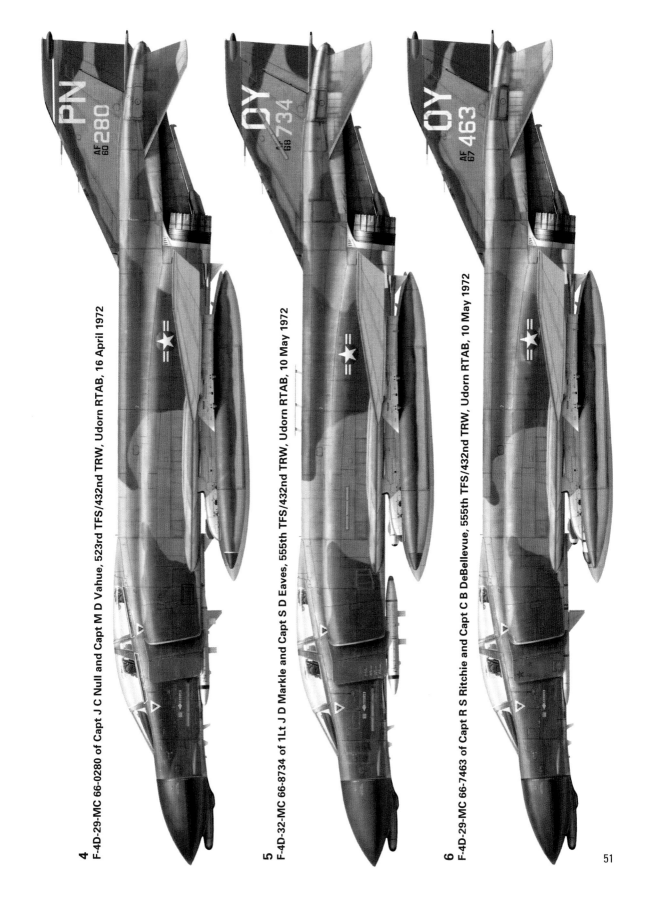

4
F-4D-29-MC 66-0280 of Capt J C Null and Capt M D Vahue, 523rd TFS/432nd TRW, Udorn RTAB, 16 April 1972

5
F-4D-32-MC 66-8734 of 1Lt J D Markle and Capt S D Eaves, 555th TFS/432nd TRW, Udorn RTAB, 10 May 1972

6
F-4D-29-MC 66-7463 of Capt R S Ritchie and Capt C B DeBellevue, 555th TFS/432nd TRW, Udorn RTAB, 10 May 1972

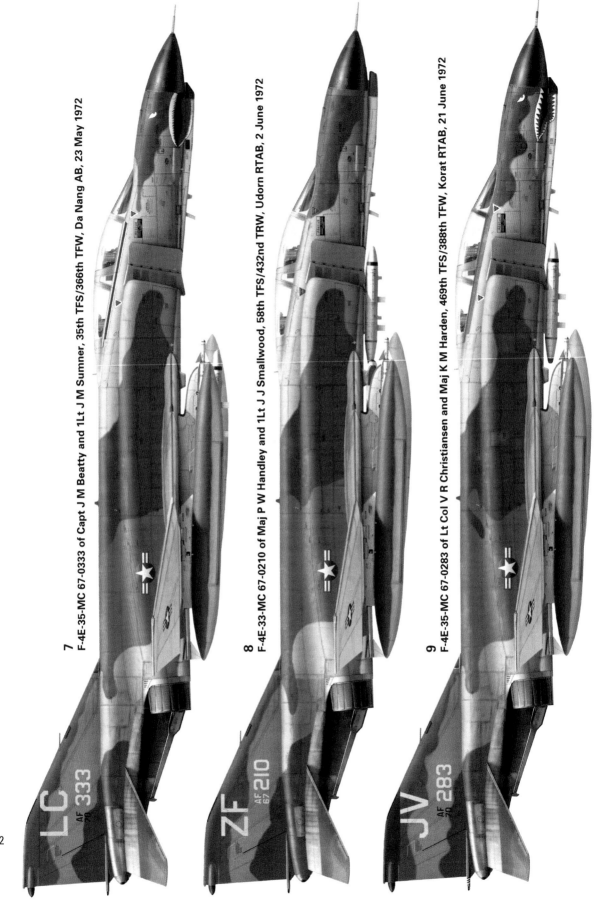

7
F-4E-35-MC 67-0333 of Capt J M Beatty and 1Lt J M Sumner, 35th TFS/366th TFW, Da Nang AB, 23 May 1972

8
F-4E-33-MC 67-0210 of Maj P W Handley and 1Lt J J Smallwood, 58th TFS/432nd TRW, Udorn RTAB, 2 June 1972

9
F-4E-35-MC 67-0283 of Lt Col V R Christiansen and Maj K M Harden, 469th TFS/388th TFW, Korat RTAB, 21 June 1972

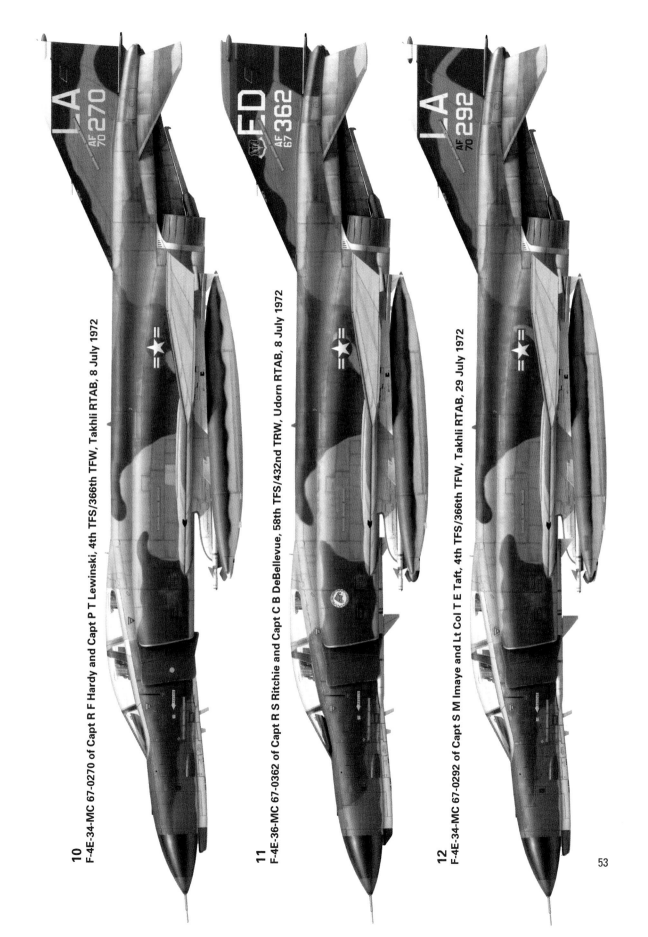

10
F-4E-34-MC 67-0270 of Capt R F Hardy and Capt P T Lewinski, 4th TFS/366th TFW, Takhli RTAB, 8 July 1972

11
F-4E-36-MC 67-0362 of Capt R S Ritchie and Capt C B DeBellevue, 58th TFS/432nd TRW, Udorn RTAB, 8 July 1972

12
F-4E-34-MC 67-0292 of Capt S M Imaye and Lt Col T E Taft, 4th TFS/366th TFW, Takhli RTAB, 29 July 1972

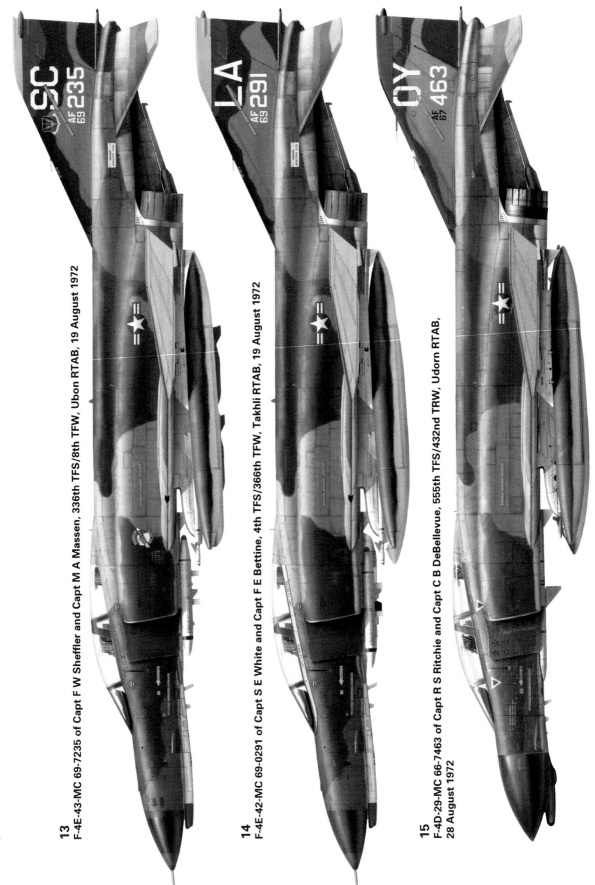

13
F-4E-43-MC 69-7235 of Capt F W Sheffler and Capt M A Massen, 336th TFS/8th TFW, Ubon RTAB, 19 August 1972

14
F-4E-42-MC 69-0291 of Capt S E White and Capt F E Bettine, 4th TFS/366th TFW, Takhli RTAB, 19 August 1972

15
F-4D-29-MC 66-7463 of Capt R S Ritchie and Capt C B DeBellevue, 555th TFS/432nd TRW, Udorn RTAB, 28 August 1972

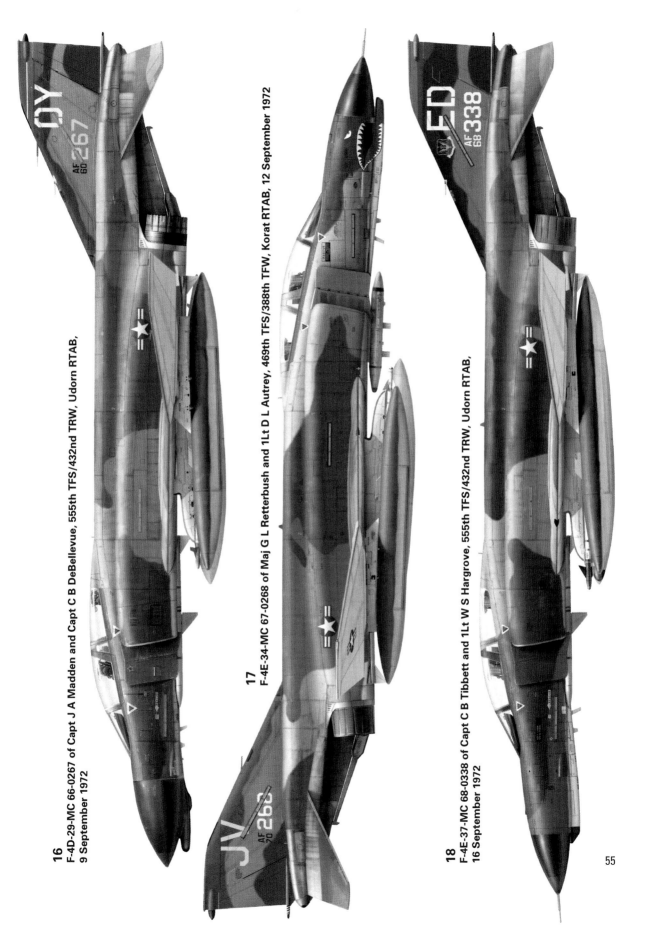

16
F-4D-29-MC 66-0267 of Capt J A Madden and Capt C B DeBellevue, 555th TFS/432nd TRW, Udorn RTAB,
9 September 1972

17
F-4E-34-MC 67-0268 of Maj G L Retterbush and 1Lt D L Autrey, 469th TFS/388th TFW, Korat RTAB, 12 September 1972

18
F-4E-37-MC 68-0338 of Capt C B Tibbett and 1Lt W S Hargrove, 555th TFS/432nd TRW, Udorn RTAB,
16 September 1972

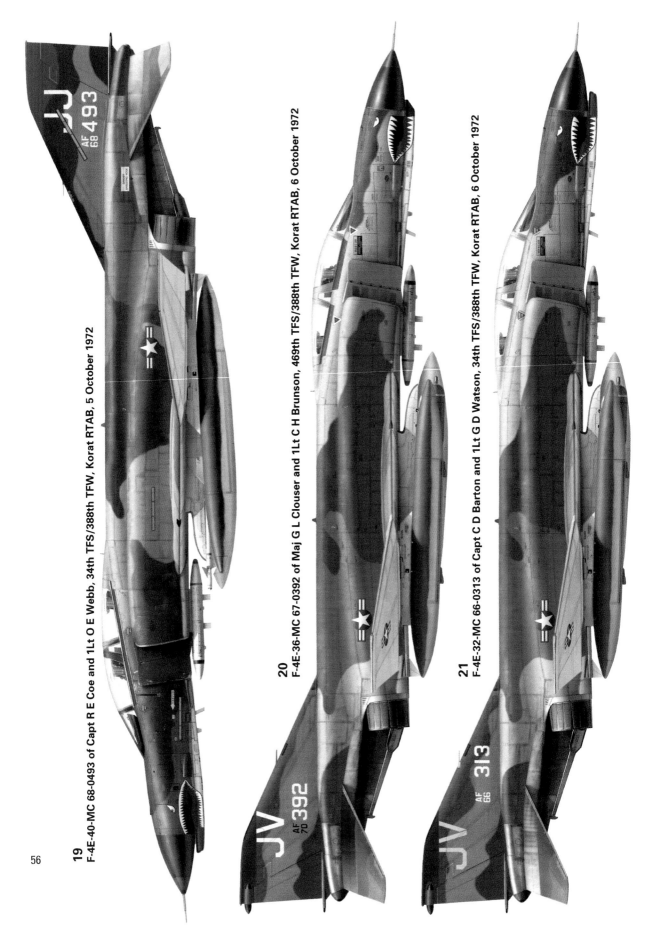

19
F-4E-40-MC 68-0493 of Capt R E Coe and 1Lt O E Webb, 34th TFS/388th TFW, Korat RTAB, 5 October 1972

20
F-4E-36-MC 67-0392 of Maj G L Clouser and 1Lt C H Brunson, 469th TFS/388th TFW, Korat RTAB, 6 October 1972

21
F-4E-32-MC 66-0313 of Capt C D Barton and 1Lt G D Watson, 34th TFS/388th TFW, Korat RTAB, 6 October 1972

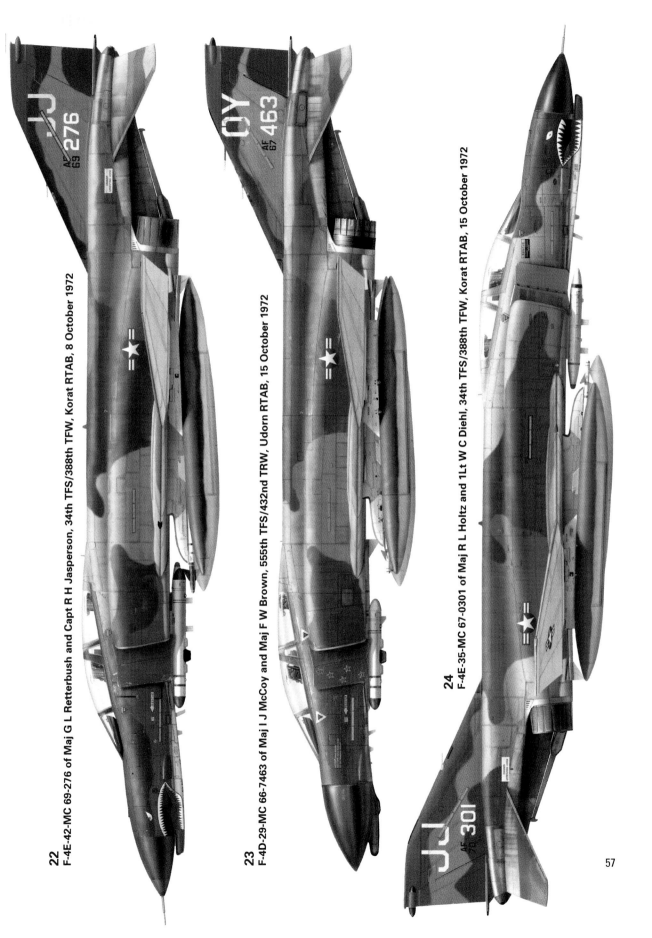

22
F-4E-42-MC 69-276 of Maj G L Retterbush and Capt R H Jasperson, 34th TFS/388th TFW, Korat RTAB, 8 October 1972

23
F-4D-29-MC 66-7463 of Maj I J McCoy and Maj F W Brown, 555th TFS/432nd TRW, Udorn RTAB, 15 October 1972

24
F-4E-35-MC 67-0301 of Maj R L Holtz and 1Lt W C Diehl, 34th TFS/388th TFW, Korat RTAB, 15 October 1972

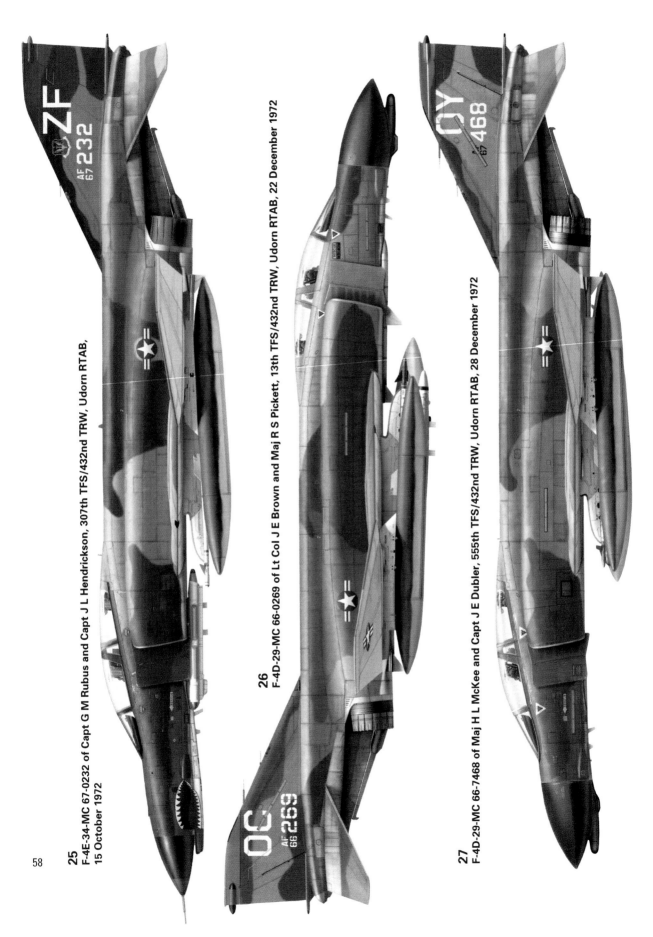

58

25
F-4E-34-MC 67-0232 of Capt G M Rubus and Capt J L Hendrickson, 307th TFS/432nd TRW, Udorn RTAB,
15 October 1972

26
F-4D-29-MC 66-0269 of Lt Col J E Brown and Maj R S Pickett, 13th TFS/432nd TRW, Udorn RTAB, 22 December 1972

27
F-4D-29-MC 66-7468 of Maj H L McKee and Capt J E Dubler, 555th TFS/432nd TRW, Udorn RTAB, 28 December 1972

1

2

3

4

5

6

7

8

9

10

11

12

13

14

15

16

17

The latter tended to operate over Route Pack IV and VIB – the Haiphong area, where the US Navy flew most of its attack missions.

Capt Madden's plan that day was to catch MiGs as they returned to Phuc Yen from own their interception efforts. His 'Olds' flight had received warning that MiGs were 50 miles out, approaching the airfield.

In the planning of the US strike, Madden had suggested a 'pincer' attack from Laos and from the sea, with a five-minute separation between the two strike components; 'We drew back to orbit near Thud

Ridge. If you got too aggressive with the MiGs, they would recover close to Hanoi instead, and there were at least 13 SAM sites around there. *Teaball* controller (Maj Barlow) had called out a MiG-21 heading west, moving towards us so we turned towards him.

'He was hard to pick up on radar, but one flight member saw him about five miles away on "short finals", with landing gear and flaps down at around 180 knots – we were blowing in at 600 knots! I fired two AIM-7s in boresight mode at low altitude, all the time trying to slow down because the guy was ready to land, but both rounds missed. We finally did get to slow down, and we approached to within 500 ft of his right side at an altitude of around 1000 ft. The guy saw us and thought, "This isn't good". He brought up his gear and flaps, engaged 'burner and accelerated out. All the time we were scissoring to try and get behind him for another shot, but you don't want to delay too much over an enemy airfield.

'Capt Bryan Tibbett ("Olds 3") said he was in place to attack, and he had an F-4E with a gun. I cleared him in to attack the MiG's "big six" (tail) and he fired two AIM-9s that both missed. The MiG then turned away from me, so I was just sitting there almost in his "six o'clock"

A replacement flap distinguishes F-4D 66-0267 OY, flown by Capts John Madden and Chuck DeBellevue for their double MiG kill on 9 September 1972. It carries AIM-9J missiles and ALQ-101 ECM and ALQ-87 pods. MiG kill markings are just visible on the splitter plate (*John Huggins via Michael France*)

A few 308th TFS jets briefly acquired nicknames in 1972, including F-4E 67-0354 *Sandi*, seen here rolling out of its Udorn revetment for a MiGCAP. The jet is loaded with AIM-9Es, AIM-7E-2s and an ALQ-101 ECM pod (*Col Bill F McDonald*)

position. I told Bryan to break off, but I don't think he heard me. He continued on in. I was sitting next to the silver MiG, and I could see Bryan's 20 mm shells going off all over the top of it. It broke away and the pilot ejected.'

Capt Tibbett and 1Lt 'Bud' Hargrove were flying a ZF-coded F-4E 'borrowed' from the TDY 308th TFS. John Madden continues;

'The flight then rejoined and headed for its MiGCAP patrol area again. Then *Teaball* called that we had bandits at 20 miles at our "six o'clock" – i.e. no threat to us. I called a 180-degree turn and we lined up on them. We were heading south, towards Hanoi, below 1000 ft at 600 knots. I offset the MiGs so that they were approaching on our left side.'

Chuck DeBellevue picked them up on radar at 15 miles, and Mike Francisco saw them shortly afterwards one mile away – a camouflaged green MiG-19 and another in aquamarine blue. John Madden again;

'Fortunately, I saw them straight away. By this time we were at 500 ft and 600 knots. We laid one hellacious turn on these guys. We'd got through about 90 degrees of turn, really pulling hard, before they saw us. They were really good pilots. They threw a turn into us, cleaned off their drop tanks and never lost formation. I was able to get off one shot (an AIM-9J – its first combat firing) but nothing seemed to happen. We were able to do a low-speed yo-yo as we continued on around, and I shot at the other guy. I never saw the missile explode, but it did hit him in the tail. He backed off his turn and rode the MiG-19 into a paddy field. The first guy we had shot at continued to come around on "Olds 3" and "4". We then went "wide open" to egress at 240 degrees, but still in formation.'

Madden's second AIM-9J had guided perfectly. Post-flight debriefing revealed that three missiles had left his jet in all, although the fate of the third was uncertain. However, the first had also done its job, exploding about 20 ft behind the first MiG-19. Intelligence sources established that the jet had caught fire as it returned to Phuc Yen and crashed on landing.

'Olds' flight then headed for home, but a radio check showed that Capt Bill Dalecky and WSO Capt Terry Murphy in 'Olds 4' were losing fuel at an alarming rate. Chuck DeBellevue reported that he had seen their aircraft take AAA damage north of Hanoi. John Madden explained;

'I gave the lead to Bryan Tibbett and told him and Bill to accelerate out so that we ("Olds 1" and "2") could cover them. A couple of other MiGs had been called airborne. The idea was to get Bill to a tanker, or at least to a point where he'd be way out in the middle of nowhere and stand a good chance of getting rescued. He soon got to 30,000 ft, and I told him to get rid of his missiles and tanks. He couldn't get a tanker, but we did get them out, and they were home that afternoon.'

Dalecky and Murphy ejected from F-4E 69-7565 (307th TFS) over Laos and were picked up by helicopter.

The AIM-9J had performed particularly well in its first combat situation, as John Madden recalled. 'I was 1000-

Capt Bryan Tibbett (right) and 1Lt Bud Hargrove (second from right) are seen at a 'Triple Nickel' briefing before their second MiG kill on 16 September 1972. Two months later, both men were killed when their *Combat Tree* F-4D (66-0501) crashed after experiencing control failure during a routine training flight over Thailand on 20 November 1972. The aircraft had shot down a MiG the previous month
(*USAF via Col R Thurlow*)

The 'Panther Pack' patch. The 35th TFS deployed to Da Nang on 1 April 1972, as Bob Jasperson wryly noted, via 'snake school' survival training in the Philippines. Its 18 F-4Ds moved to Korat on 12 June 1972 under 388th TFW control. Bob's MiG kill (with Gary Retterbush) came at the end of the deployment. '10 October was our last day for combat so that we could get the jets ready for the flight back to Kunsan. As squadron admin officer, I told the schedulers I couldn't fly after 8 October. I therefore knew the mission that day would be my last' (*Bob Jasperson*)

Photographed on 11 October 1972 – the day before the 35th TFS returned to Kunsan from Korat – this scoreboard records the squadron's six air-to-air and eight air-to-ground kills. Two others (Young/Claiborne and Lippemeir/Nelson) remained unconfirmed. Maj Lueders' six 'ground' kills were achieved in multiple CBU passes on MiG bases, taking heavy AAA all the way. Lt Col Ferguson (named on the canopy frame) took over from Lt Col Lyle Beckers as CO. When the squadron returned to Kunsan, he led a flight made up entirely of MiG killer crews (*via Bob Jasperson*)

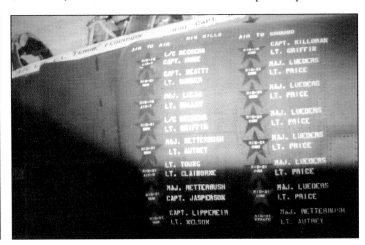

2000 ft behind the MiG, pulling 6g. An AIM-9E was only good for 3g'. Short supply meant that AIM-9Js initially appeared only on Udorn's flight lead aircraft (usually F-4Ds), while F-4Es in the two 'wingman' positions usually had AIM-9Es. Flight and element lead aircraft also typically had four AIM-7E-2 Sparrows, three drop tanks, a 'short' ALQ-101 ECM pod and an ALQ-89 missile beacon jammer.

Three days later the 388th TFW also despatched a trio of MiG-21s, two of them being destroyed by F-4Es from 'Finch' chaff escort flight near Kep airfield. A MiG warning was transmitted via *Teaball*, but it was not received clearly enough for the MiGs' potential target to be identified. The escorts therefore remained in place, rather than turning to engage a possible threat, but they eventually saw two MiG-21s approaching from their rear. The F-4s turned to block the attack, but both MiGs pressed on and hit F-4E 69-7266 in the chaff formation with an 'Atoll'. WSO Capt Rudy Zuberbuhler, flying his 368th combat mission, and Capt Fred McMurray parachuted into captivity from their blazing aircraft.

A 4th TFW F-4E (69-0288) had been shot down in similar circumstances the previous day, its crew, pilot Capt Brian Ratzlaff and WSO Capt Jerome Heeren, whose combined combat experience totalled 712 missions, also becoming PoWs. 'Finch 1', flown by 35th TFS boss Lt Col Lyle 'Sky King' Beckers and 1Lt Thomas Griffin, immediately pursued the MiG-21 (flown by six-kill ace Nguyen Tien Sam) as it lined up on Zuberbuhler's F-4. They fired two AIM-7s which both failed. Beckers then followed up quickly with a pair of AIM-9Es, and the second of these impacted on the MiG's left wing, causing a huge fire. He then selected 'guns' and fired out most of his 20 mm rounds at the enemy fighter. Further explosions racked the MiG as it dived away steeply in flames.

Meanwhile, 'Finch 3', flown by Maj Gary Retterbush and 1Lt Dan Autrey, had taken on the second MiG-21. Once again, a pair of AIM-7s was launched, but neither guided successfully. Three AIM-9Es were then fired, and although all of them passed close to the VPAF jet, they inflicted no damage. Proving the effectiveness of the M61 gun once again, Maj Retterbush closed on the MiG and fired 350 rounds of 20 mm at it, scoring hits all over the fighter, and apparently incapacitating the pilot. The aircraft pulled up into a stall, with the pilot slumped in his ejection seat, then fell away on fire.

The third kill on 12 September took place later that day. 'Robin' flight, also from the 388th TFW, was escorting a strike flight against the Tuan Quan railway bridge when two MiG-21s struck from behind the formation. 'Robin 1' loosed off an AIM-7 out of parameters to distract the VPAF pilots and then went after a MiG-21 as it broke away to avoid the Sparrow. A second AIM-7E was fired and this missed, as did three AIM-9Es that the 'Robin' leader also released.

35th TFS personnel show how comfortable a Da Nang F-4D could be. Most at ease in the front seat is squadron CO, and double MiG killer, Lt Col Lyle 'Sky King' Beckers. Fellow MiG killer Bob Jasperson is second left in the top row. Maj Ernie Lueders (third from right in the front row) claimed six MiGs destroyed on the ground. Maj Bill Kyle (third from left, standing) was wingman pilot on Retterbush and Jasperson's MiG kill mission. Most squadron jets carried the designated UP tailcodes, to which 'yours' was often added in small black letters below the code. Alternatively, the word 'tits' was sometimes inscribed above UP. However, the significance of the *Lil' Porky Pig* nickname on the splitter plate remains unknown. 66-7621 later became a 366th TFW 'Fast FAC' jet, and it was shot down by AAA on 26 May 1972 while controlling an air strike (*via Bob Jasperson*)

The initiative then shifted to 'Robin 2' when a second MiG passed at close quarters between the F-4s and the lead MiG, heading off to their right. Capt Michael Mahaffey and 1Lt George Shields, in F-4D 65-0608 ('Robin 2'), turned to follow it. They fired a single AIM-9E that guided efficiently and exploded in the MiG's tail section. It began a long spin to the ground near Yen Bai airbase, shedding parts and debris.

TWO SECONDS

The final decisive duel of September brought the second kill in a week for Bryan Tibbett and Bud Hargrove. Once again, *Teaball* suffered from a technical problem, so control of the interception passed to *Red Crown* and *Disco*. Tibbett flew 'Chevy 3' in a 555th TFS MiGCAP, using a 58th TFS F-4E (68-0338) that had already downed a MiG-21 in May 1972. Bryan Tibbett was the second most experienced pilot in the unit at the time with 350 hours on the F-4. 'Chevy' flight leader John Madden brought 1200 hours of Phantom II experience to his role that day, but he and his WSO Mike Hilliard were let down by missile technology.

Cleared to pursue a single MiG-21 that was heading south-east along the course of the Red River, Tibbett took over the lead after all eight of 'Chevy 1's' missiles had failed. He too had little success with the AIM-9J at first. Two didn't guide, one failed to detonate and the last, fired at a height of just 50 ft, hit the MiG in its tail section. Its pilot began a desperate, last minute turn, but his elevator system was destroyed and his fighter dived into the ground seconds after he had ejected. Only one of the AIM-9Js fired in that combat had worked successfully, and it was subsequently discovered that the missile's test programme had never included low-altitude launches like those used by 'Chevy' flight.

BACKING THE 'BUFFS'

The air war gained momentum once again in October 1972 with heavy attacks on four VPAF airfields on the first day of the month that destroyed at least five MiGs and saw some aggressive attacks by defending VPAF fighters. Many missiles were fired ineffectively by both sides, and only one F-4 was damaged by an 'Atoll'. The following day the MiGs were equally determined, four MiG-21s and two MiG-19s breaking through to attack LGB-carrying F-4s while the MiGCAPs were manoeuvring to elude a barrage of SAMs. All but one of the bomber flights had to jettison their weapons, although no aircraft were lost.

The pressure was maintained on 5 October when two MiG-21s launched from Kep airbase to oppose F-4s attacking munitions storage near Yen Bai. A 335th TFS F-4D (66-8738) was shot down, allegedly by ace Nguyen Tien Sam, who had survived being shot down himself on 12 September. 'Robin' flight, from the 34th TFS at Korat RTAFB, was one of the support flights, led by Capt Richard Coe and 1Lt Ken Webb III. After his Number 2 and 3 flight members had to return to base, Coe and Webb were left with 'Robin 4', flown by Capts Dave Ladd and George Sebren – an inexperienced crew on TDY from the 48th TFW at RAF Lakenheath, in the UK.

Two MiGs were reported to be heading for them as they neared their initial point for the attack, and shortly afterwards their LGB flight saw two enemy fighters high and off to their right side, close to the Chinese

307th TFS F-4E 67-0240 sits in its revetment at Udorn in the summer of 1972 armed with two Paveway I LGBs – a vital new precision weapon in the *Linebacker* campaign (*Col Bill McDonald*)

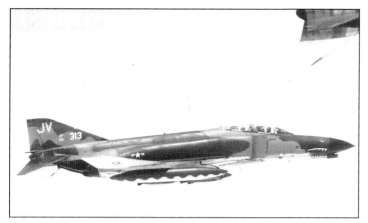

F-4E 66-0313 in the 34th TFS markings that it wore for its 6 October 1972 MiG-19 kill (*via A Collishaw*)

border. They were also warned of another pair approaching 'in the dark' – i.e. at very low altitude. As the strike formation began to turn towards the reported MiGs, one of the strike crews saw MiG-21s and cleaned off his ordnance load. Dick Coe jettisoned his fuel tanks, although one damaged an aileron as it left its pylon, and engaged afterburner.

Circling to try and catch sight of the MiGs, he soon noticed a MiG-21 about three miles out in front. His speed had built up to Mach 1.6 during his descending spirals, so he was able to rapidly close on the MiG. 1Lt Webb selected 'auto-acquisition' on their radar and Coe fired a single AIM-7E-2, but immediately afterwards received an unspecific warning of MiGs at 'someone's "six o'clock"'. He had intended to follow up with an AIM-9, as he did not trust the AIM-7, but instead he had to barrel roll up so as to 'check six'.

Looking ahead again, he saw a large, black smoke cloud with two streaks of white vapour emerging from it. Seconds later another MiG warning from Ken Webb forced the crew into a high-g turn as two more MiGs (the ones that had approached at low level) passed close overhead. Further attempts at interception were ruled out by Dave Ladd's fuel state, so 'Robin' flight headed home.

The 'post mortem' initially suggested that 'Robin 1' might have finished off both MiGs with a single shot, hence the two white smoke trails. However, another flight's debriefing revealed that the MiG had been seen to break into two parts and a wing had fallen away, making a second trail of fuel and smoke. Their kill was the first for the 34th TFS, but two more followed in quick succession.

Maj Gordon Clouser was among a number of ex-F-105 pilots who believed that a fighter wasn't a fighter unless it had a gun. Consequently, he preferred the F-4E, although he also flew F-4Ds from the 35th TFS that were at Korat RTAFB on detachment from Kunsan AB's 3rd TFW. In-theatre politics gave the F-4Ds the air-to-ground role, while the E-models got the MiGCAP missions. It was a 35th TFS 'Rams' F-4E (67-0392) that he and 1Lt Cecil Brunson flew on 6 October 1972, with Capt Charles Barton and 1Lt George Watson in the wingman slot, flying F-4E 66-0313 as 'Eagle 4'.

The other two jets in this hunter-killer team were F-105Gs armed with anti-radiation missiles, while the F-4Es carried two AIM-7s, four AIM-9s and four CBU-52s to attack SAM sites. Gordon Clouser explained;

'Occasionally, we carried the smaller CBU-58 canisters, but CBU-52 was the preferred ordnance for SA-2 sites. The *Wild Weasel* F-105s would typically fire their missiles first, and when the flight was within visual range of the site (identified by the F-105's missile detonations), the F-4s would deliver ordnance. The two F-105 crews rather enjoyed having their own personal MiGCAP as part of their flight.

The CBU-24 canisters carried by
307th TFS F-4E 69-7579 suggest
that it is taxying out from Udorn
at the start of yet another highly
dangerous *Iron Hand* anti-SAM
mission in the late summer of 1972
(*Col Bill F McDonald*)

'Receiving warning of approaching MiGs, the F-105s, as pre-briefed, turned away from the threat area when it became apparent that the MiGs were closing in on us. The F-4Es turned towards the threat, hoping to "paint" the MiGs on radar. We made at least one more turn at an altitude of around 8000 ft before gaining visual contact. It's amazing how easily a sharp-eyed aviator can pick out aircraft – until one tries to look ahead, left, right, up and down at the same time, knowing that you are someone else's target.

'We didn't see the MiGs – a silver-grey MiG-19 and a sky-blue MiG-21 – until they were almost line abreast (staggered one behind the other) on our left side, and perhaps 1000 ft above, on a reciprocal heading. I called a hard left turn into the threat and my wingman crossed from right to left during the turn. We then jettisoned tanks and ordnance and continued turning to the left, but descending too, since we had lost visual contact with the threat and needed to gain airspeed.

'My wingman never obtained visual contact with the MiGs and, thinking he was in imminent danger, rolled left into a vertical dive while I continued my left, descending turn. As we "bottomed out" at 200 ft, the MiG-19 impacted the ground in a vertical dive, roughly 500 ft off my left wing. An agency that monitored radio communications later stated that the pilot had yelled the Vietnamese equivalent of "Oh, shit!" just prior to impact. At the time of this crash we were flying at just over 500 knots, but not going in the same direction as the MiG-19.'

Col Clouser attributed the VPAF pilot's error of judgement to 'target fixation'.

'I then spotted the MiG-21 at our "eight o'clock" position, so I continued the left turn, while climbing hard and pulling the nose back down to get behind him. The solid blue colour of this MiG is one of my main impressions of the entire engagement. As the MiG-21 bottomed out of his descending turn, he reversed direction, turned right and flew into low-lying clouds that were hanging above the karst rock formations.

'Rather than try to find him in the clouds so close to the ground, and with my chief concern being re-constitution of the flight, I continued my turn to a westerly heading, saw my wingman ahead of me at low altitude and quickly joined up with him. Less than 30 seconds later we were surprised to see our two F-105Gs completing a 360-degree turn in the hope of giving us a chance to rejoin them. We came together smoothly in formation as if it had been planned that way. It couldn't have happened better if we had tried!'

The flight egressed on the deck for an uneventful return to base, where each F-4 crew was awarded a half-kill for the MiG-19 on the basis that they had 'manoeuvred' it into the ground. It was the last MiG-19 to be destroyed from the few survivors of the original batch of 59. MiG-19 operations ceased shortly afterwards.

Maj Gary Retterbush and 1Lt Dan Autrey flew F-4E-34-MC 67-0268 for Retterbush's first MiG kill on 12 September. The following month the 469th TFS (JV codes) deactivated at Korat and the F-4Es assumed the JJ code of the 34th TFS (*via J T Thompson*)

Two days later Maj Gary Retterbush was credited with a second kill while leading a 35th TFS strike escort flight, with Capt Bob Jasperson as WSO. Bob had been a C-141 navigator before being assigned to the F-4 via the McDill AFB RTU and a posting to Kunsan AB. He recalled;

'By the time I got into F-4s, the official job title was already WSO, although 90 per cent of the time we were called "GIB", even among ourselves. Some of the pilots with previous single-seat experience didn't necessarily appreciate sharing their missions with a non-pilot. I was also a civilian pilot, which maybe made it easier for them to accept.

'I was in the lead F-4 ("Lark 1"), and everything was fine until it was time to take to the runway. The locking mechanism on my canopy would not fully engage. You were not supposed to force canopies closed because the ejection system might not function properly. Finally, on the third try I pulled down on both sides of the canopy and it locked. We got airborne at 1419 hrs local time and headed for our pre-strike tanker, "Red 155", at flight level 185. On the way, one of the wingmen had to abort. We didn't fly as three-ships, so we sent the other wingman back home and pressed on as a two-ship with "Lark 3". We were escorting three flights of four-ships – "Beech" flight, which made a level LORAN drop from flight level 200, plus two Ubon flights ("Date" and "Pine"), which made standard dive-bombing passes.

'While we were with the tanker, we switched our radios to *Disco*'s frequency. My pilot told the controller to give us close-in vectors on any MiG that got within 20 to 25 miles of our flights. We dropped off the tanker at 1518 hrs local time with a "time-on-target" of 1545 hrs. We spread out, line abreast, behind the three attack flights.

'Soon after we crossed into North Vietnam at 1525 hrs, *Disco* started calling out the position of a bandit. It was heading north at first, then west and then more to the south. We were at 20,000-24,000 ft when we picked up a MiG-21 visually. I got one quick glimpse of it as it passed our "ten o'clock" at one mile. It was silver, with red markings. The jet slid right in front of us and behind "Pine" flight. I never saw it again because I had my head down in the radarscope trying to get a lock-on to it.

'Maj Retterbush was in afterburner closing on the MiG. "Pine" jettisoned their bombs and broke left. The MiG broke to the right and dived. With all the ground-clutter on the radarscope, I was unable to lock on. Retterbush called for boresight mode, and he was able to lock on using the 'auto-acquisition' switch on the throttles. He got the MiG in his optical sight and had a good tone from the first AIM-9. He squeezed and held the trigger, but nothing happened, so he "stepped" to the next Sidewinder with the same result. Finally, since we had closed on the MiG quite a bit, he selected guns. During this time the MiG had reversed his turn to the left and then back to the right. I believe he had lost sight of us.

'Maj Retterbush fired a short burst and the tracers went just aft of the MiG's tail, or so I'm told. My attention, after going into boresight mode, was completely directed behind us. Once my pilot had the target in sight, or we had a good

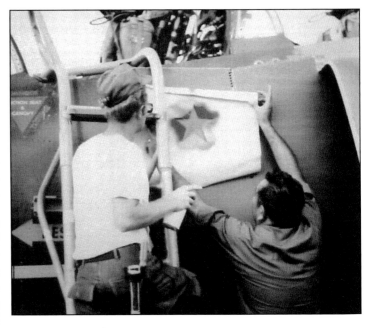

The crew chief of F-4E 69-0276 sprays a MiG kill star onto the jet's splitter plate for Gary Retterbush and Bob Jasperson on 8 October. This aircraft was in turn shot down just four days later by MiG-21 ace Nguyen Duc Soat, with Capt Myron Young and MiG killer 1Lt Cecil Brunson being taken prisoner (*Bob Jasperson*)

lock-on, my job was to clear our rear position, and that of our wingman. As the gun fired, I was looking back to our "seven o'clock", where our wingman was, to make sure we weren't being followed by another bandit. Maj Retterbush pulled the gunsight just ahead of the MiG and fired a second, short burst that went into its fuselage and fuel tanks. The MiG immediately started to burn and the pilot ejected successfully.

'The time was 1544 hrs local, and we had descended to about 11,000 ft, probably at around 500-550 knots. We circled the area once and managed to see the MiG's wreckage burning on the ground through a hole in the cloud layer. *Disco* reported no other bandits in the area, and all attack flights had egressed to the west, so we headed out.

'We didn't need to refuel at the tankers so we headed back. It was customary to do a victory roll over the base after a kill. The most g we pulled on the entire mission was in the pull-up for our victory roll! After we landed we examined the two AIM-9s that we had tried to fire. The electrical power units on each missile had fired, as witnessed by the exhaust stains on the sides, but neither had launched.'

Bob Jasperson's F-4E (69-0276) was shot down on 12 October by an 'Atoll' fired by Nguyen Duc Soat for his sixth, and final, claim. The crew, who were both captured, included 1Lt Cecil Brunson who had scored a MiG kill with Gordon Clouser earlier that month.

The cockpit teamwork employed by Retterbush and Jasperson was typical of the routines that most crews devised to maximise the advantages of the F-4's two-man cockpit. Each WSO had his own sub-routines too. For example, radar scan patterns would be set up differently depending on the aircraft's position within its flight so that maximum radar coverage could be provided by the four Phantom IIs. WSOs in the lead aircraft (1 and 3) tended to spend more time on radar work, setting up targets for their "shooter" pilots, whereas wingman WSOs looked out of the cockpit a lot more to provide visual 'situational awareness' for the flight as a whole.

There was also the radio to monitor on the strike frequency used by the formation, with occasional checks on 'guard' frequency to catch any emergency situations, rescue beepers etc. RHAW (Radar Homing And Warning) gear also had to be monitored, although many crews turned the volume on this and 'guard' down or off so that they could give full attention to the strike frequency. The ECM pods carried on most missions were of minor concern for most flyers, as Mike Cooper explained;

'The people who were involved with the pods re-tuned them periodically depending on what "intel" was telling them. They were playing games with them every day, but this was technology that we didn't care about, although we were briefed on it. If we were flying air-to-air missions we didn't worry about the pods because we found that the enemy were pretty disciplined about not shooting SAMs when MiGs were operating.'

Capt John Madden and WSO Capt Larry Pettit destroyed another MiG-21 on 12 October – Madden's third and Pettit's second. John Madden recalled;

'The sortie had been delayed. It was supposed to have been a morning mission. We had received some "intel" that there were going to be a lot of MiGs up that day. In the end, mine was the only air-to-air flight ("Vega"). We were the first in, to block the MiGs from getting to the bombers. They were using their "trail" tactic then'.

Larry Pettit continues;

'The weather was terrible, and after a while we positioned ourselves between the MiGs and the strike force. I remember hearing a beeper that was later determined to be from an F-4 (Capt Myron Young and 1Lt Cecil Brunson's 69-0276), shot down somewhere below us. Because of the beeper's interference with the calls from *Red Crown*, I deselected "guard" channel.'

John Madden again;

'The MiGs came in a big, clockwise circle. We just kept pointing at them as a blocking force, but we could never get a lock-on to a MiG. One went past us – Larry saw him at our "eleven o'clock", head on at 25,000 ft. He blew through us, but I knew he would be turning left because all the action was that way'.

Larry Pettit recalled;

'We passed canopy-to-canopy, and I observed the "gomer" looking at us as we were looking at him. I kept him in sight while John, also keeping him in view, manoeuvred the aircraft in a right turn to get below and behind him. The MiG then manoeuvred, as it seemed to me, straight up. He then did a split and went 80-90 degrees straight down.'

John Madden added;

'I had got inside his turn and overshot him a little. He saw me as I was trying to "S-turn" to get behind him. He got nervous at that and went into afterburner, rolled over and went straight down in a 60-70 degree dive. We entered a thin cloud base at 20,000 ft and were several thousand feet behind him trying to get lined up.

'There was undercast at about 9000 ft, and he entered this, going almost straight down. I pulled my flight up just above the undercast – the terrain rose to more than 3000 ft in that area. I think that in his attempt

Capts Al Becker, Ed Allen and Keith Jones and Lt Col Griff Baily congratulate Capt Jeff Feinstein (left) on becoming the USAF's third ace after his fifth MiG kill on 13 October 1972. His pilot on this occasion was squadron commander Lt Col Westphal. Keith Jones recalled that, '"Olds" flight was loaded with aerial combat experience that day because we were determined that Jeff should get his fifth MiG, but he needed no help. Jeff was an absolutely superb WSO whose skill and bravery led to his ace status. He worked with *Red Crown* to achieve an incredibly efficient vector, tracking solution and missile launch. It's a good thing he did because Ed and I spotted at least three other MiG-21s in the immediate area preparing to engage us in one hell of a dogfight if Jeff had taken much longer. As it was, we observed the missile impact, immediately egressed the area and came home to a great celebration' (*Lt Col Keith Jones*)

F-4D-29-MC 66-7501 was the mount for Jeff Feinstein's fifth kill, flown with his highly respected squadron CO, Lt Col Curtis Westphal. The aircraft previously flew with the 8th TFW during *Rolling Thunder* (*via Peter Schinkelshoek*)

to get away he lost situational awareness, and couldn't recover from the dive. Intelligence sources said he went straight into the ground.'

Larry Pettit concluded the saga;

'We had a meeting on tactics to attend at Da Nang, so we proceeded to the tanker and then on to the South Vietnamese base. When we landed, we were met with champagne (which we couldn't drink!) and congratulations, and we were informed of the crash of the MiG. John always called this his "cost effective kill".'

Jeff Feinstein's final MiG was downed on 13 October in a 13th TFS F-4D (66-7501), piloted by 43-year-old Lt Col Curtis Westphal. It made him the USAF's third ace of the war, and the second WSO ace. On his wing were Ed Allen ('Olds 2'), with WSO Keith 'Bill' Jones, who described the combat as 'short and sweet – it was textbook'.

Feinstein's first radar contact was established at 17 miles, and confirmed as bandits. His *Combat Tree* could have enabled a BVR missile launch, but Lt Col Westphal had to forego this because of friendly aircraft in the area. They waited until visual contact was established at one mile, turned left to engage and fired three AIM-7E-2s. Every 'Olds' flight member saw the second missile hit the MiG in its aft section, causing an immediate conflagration. Seconds later its pilot ejected, and the blazing wreck disappeared into the undercast.

Lt Col Westphal described the attack to the Udorn base newspaper, *Easy Flyer*, at the time;

'The missiles went squiggling on out and it looked like a race to see which one was going to get there first. They impacted near his tail section. The MiG started trailing fuel like a light contrail. A few seconds later the

Fully armed and ready to go, this well-laden 34th TFS F-4E (67-0230) awaits the arrival of its crew in its Korat revetment (*Don Jay*)

aeroplane exploded and part of the right wing came off. He went into an almost vertical dive and we saw the seat come flying out.'

Commenting on the fact that Jeff Feinstein wore glasses, he said, 'Don't let those glasses fake you out – I think they're telescopes'!

The F-4D used for this engagement was lost over Thailand when a control failure occurred during a training sortie on 20 November 1972. Tragically, double MiG killers Bryan Tibbett and 'Bud' Hargrove died in the resulting crash.

BATTLING ON

Numerous MiGs were encountered on 15 October in one of the largest aerial battles prior to President Nixon's announcement of a suspension of bombing from 22 October. Maj Lon Holtz and 1Lt William Diehl claimed the last 34th TFS (and 388th TFW) victory during a strike near Viet Tri by Ubon-based F-4 flights.

Holtz was element leader in 'Parrot' escort flight, which was vectored by *Red Crown* towards two MiG-21s dead ahead of them. The bandits were sighted at two miles, and they streaked overhead on a reciprocal course seconds later. 'Parrot' lead decided to let them go, and the flight reverted to its close escort role. 'Parrot 4' then saw, and turned towards, another MiG-21 which also vanished into clouds.

The strike flights had pushed on ahead by this time, so Maj Holtz elected to fly orbits near Viet Tri, covering the strikers as they egressed. In so doing, his element attempted to engage two more MiG-21s, again with no outcome. The next 'intruders' were 'Buick' flight from Udorn,

A monsoon downpour could not be allowed to stop the work at Udorn, even though rain was literally bouncing off the F-4's canopy and drenching the groundcrew who were starting up its engines (*Col Bill F McDonald*)

F-4E 67-0301 was a MiG killer for Maj Lon Holtz and 1Lt William Diehl. The jet remained in 34th TFS service until late 1974 (*R F Dorr via Alan Howarth*)

This photograph serves as a reminder that the 432nd TRW flew three different Phantom II variants in October 1972. Lining up at the start of a reconnaissance mission over North Vietnam are a 14th TRS RF-4C, a 308th TFS F-4E and a 555th TFS F-4D (*USAF via Col R Thurlow*)

who charged through the circling 'Parrot' flight in pursuit of yet another MiG-21. As he regrouped with his wingman, Maj Holtz saw a parachute at 4000 ft. As it was white rather than yellow, he assumed it could be from an F-4, so he carefully noted its position. Moving closer, he saw a MiG-21 making a right turn around the floating parachute.

While the MiG pilot was distracted by what later proved to be one of his own squadron pilots beneath the 'chute, Holtz closed to 3000 ft and fired an AIM-9E. The missile plunged into the MiG's jet-pipe and blew off large chunks of the tail. It dived away, blazing furiously.

The other two MiG kills that day added to the 432nd TRW's total. Capts Gary Rubus and James Hendrickson were credited with a MiG-21 as 'Buick 3' in the flight that passed through 'Parrot' flight's orbit. It was probably the parachute from their MiG kill that Maj Holtz observed. 'Buick' was an ingress CAP tasked, as Jim Hendrickson explained, 'to engage the MiGs before they got into position to attack the strike

A 308th TFS F-4E returns to Ubon with empty racks while another prepares for its mission. The Air America T-28 (left) was also resident at the base (*Col Bill F McDonald*)

flight'. He and Gary Rubus were a 307th TFS crew detached from the 31st TFW, and were well prepared for MiG fighting;

'The 31st TFW was the first unit to host the newly-formed T-38A aggressor unit in the USA, so both the 307th and 308th TFSs had some dissimilar air-to-air training before the *Linebacker* deployment. On top of that, both Gary and I had completed the FWS course at Nellis AFB in August 1971 before deploying. This included intensive air-to-air training. I don't remember getting a lot of information on *Rolling Thunder*, but we were getting MiG engagement reports in the period up to deployment, some of which must have come from *Rolling Thunder*.'

The 307th TFS, commanded by Lt Col Robert M Sweet, arrived at Udorn in five increments between 15 July and 12 August 1972, replacing the 308th TFS. The squadron logged 1000 missions in its first three months as 'summer help' to the 'Triple Nickels'.

Jim Hendrickson described their MiG kill;

'The call we received (from *Red Crown*) told us there were two MiG-21s – "blue" bandits – airborne from Phuc Yen. Seconds later we received a second call that the bandits were headed in our direction. Then a third announced that they were 16 miles away at 3000 ft. We headed in their direction and picked up two returns on our radar, then we locked on to the lead aircraft.'

Capt Bob Summers and WSO Capt Randy Case (posing with a jungle knife in his teeth) set off for work over the North. Their 307th TFS F-4E-45-MC (69-7579) carries an impressive load of CBU-24, which probably indicates that the crew were about to undertake a hazardous SAM-site strike (*Col Bill McDonald*)

Capts Rubus and Hendrickson unstrap from F-4E 67-0232 after their MiG kill mission on 15 October 1972 (*via Jim Hendrickson*)

Capt Gary Rubus, TSgt Wells (307th TFS gun shop – Rubus had downed the MiG-21 with the F-4's cannon), Sgt Rodriguez (67-0232's crew chief) and Capt Hendrickson pose for a photograph after their MiG kill (*via Jim Hendrickson*)

The initial attack on the MiGs was by 'Buick 1', flown by Lt Col Carl Funk and Maj James Malaney, but the radar in their *Combat Tree* F-4D broke lock twice. Jim Hendrickson explained;

'The F-4 radar, whatever the variant, wasn't supposed to be able to track a "look down, shoot down" target. We were the only ones in the flight able to track the target. We were lucky to have a radar that was better "tweaked" than the others, and it would happily track a target below us in ground clutter.'

'Buick 1' cleared Rubus's F-4E to fire instead;

'At this time we were at 2100 ft, and we hit clouds. We dumped fuel tanks and pressed on at supersonic speed. Four miles later we fired an AIM-7E (we carried two "non-dogfight" Sparrows, four AIM-9Es and two ECM pods in the forward missile wells), but it detonated prematurely in front of the aircraft. The missile was fired at about 650 knots, closing at 300 knots on the target. The explosion must have caught the MiG pilot's attention because he turned his aircraft our way. Our wingman fired a few 20 mm rounds at him just as the second MiG broke out from the clouds.

'We turned through the clouds at 4500 ft and fired a second missile (at about 400 knots and a range of 4500 ft) but it didn't guide. I could see

F-4E 67-0232, as flown by Capts Gary Rubus and Jim Hendrickson (with 307th TFS codes) for the MiG kill recorded on its intake. WSO Jim recalled that, 'You could hear and feel the vibration of the gun firing and you could feel a distinct thump under your feet when an AIM-7 kicked away from the belly upon being launched'. Both men were well prepared for aerial combat. 'The 31st TFW was the first unit in the USA to host the T-38A Aggressors, so both the 307th and 308th TFS had some dissimilar air-to-air training. Both Gary and I had completed the FWS course at Nellis in August 1971, which included intensive air-to-air training' (*Norm Taylor*)

the MiG as we came out through the clouds, and suggested to Capt Rubus that we should fire an AIM-9E. He said he thought he could get it with the nose gun.

'The gun attack took place in a near-vertical dive, in afterburner at about Mach 0.95 just as the MiG neared the bottom of his dive. Rubus fired at 1100 ft and again at 800 ft, seeing cannon shell explosions on the silver jet with its thin green camouflage. We saw the MiG pilot eject as his aeroplane rolled off to the left. We pulled right, and could see the MiG smoking and finally crashing into a small valley. At just about that time we received a call that there were three other MiGs on our tail, so we made a rapid exit.'

The entire fight took less than three minutes, during which time the strike flights had been forced to go to their secondary target – Yen Bai airfield – where they destroyed or damaged several MiGs. They came under continual attack, and it was the third MiGCAP, 'Chevy', that fought off the assailants. No F-4s were lost, despite heavy opposition.

'Chevy' lead was Maj Ivy McCoy, with WSO Maj Fred Brown. Their aircraft was F-4D 66-7463. McCoy recalled;

'This aircraft was available because Steve Ritchie had finally got his fifth MiG and could go home. After he got his third MiG, he flew '463 as a MiGCAP leader until the Air Force had themselves an ace. He was visibly relieved when he finally got number five. After that, the other squadrons got the MiGCAP lead in turn.'

On 15 October 66-7463 had a sixth star added to its splitter plate after McCoy and Brown made the third kill that day. Ivy McCoy continues;

'I was "Chevy" lead in '463 with *Combat Tree*. My WSO thought this device was "the berries", but I can't say I was impressed by it. It certainly didn't play an important role that day. I was in the second wave of MiGCAP F-4s for a mission in the Hanoi area. When we dropped off the tanker and switched to "mission primary" frequency, we could hear that the MiGs were up, and that "Buick" flight had already got one.'

Rubus and Hendrickson had shot down their MiG and their 'Buick' flight had then left, allowing 'Chevy' to fill the CAP space. *Red Crown* called that more MiGs were rising from Phuc Yen, and the controller vectored 'Chevy' to their altitude of 12,000 ft. Ivy McCoy had no visual contact, and he continued on the vector until the radar plots merged;

'We passed the MiGs head-on, but they were in the clouds. We had already begun a hard 180-degree turn, but not soon enough. More vectors brought us to the vicinity of the strike flights. Amid the confusion, my number three, Capt Glenn Profitt, said that he had a MiG in sight. I gave him the lead, but his sighting turned out to be incorrect, so I took back the lead. Glenn didn't acknowledge this, and he later chased the same MiG downhill as I did, but I got him first!

'At about that time I saw contrails, and *Red Crown* said they were "my MiGs". My wingman, Col Robert Wayne (in a PN-coded F-4D) called "bandits" at "two o'clock". They descended right in front of me as luck would have it, and I executed a hard right turn. Maj Brown kept trying to get a lock-on. Since I had the MiG in my inner gunsight reticle and, according to the McDonnell Douglas people, that meant enough continuous wave energy from the F-4's radar for the AIM-7 to guide, I started firing AIM-7s over a 23-second period. Three missiles came off

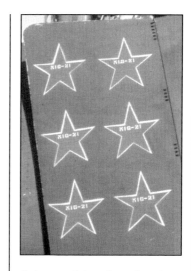

A close up of the splitter plate of legendary 432nd TRW F-4D 66-7463, as marked at Udorn in early 1973 (*Col R Thurlow*)

'Summer Help' TDY units at Udorn often felt sidelined, as their activities did not count in the permanently based wing's operational statistics, so they were therefore low in the 'food chain'. For a mere 80 cents, 308th TFS personnel could buy this patch to express their feelings (*Col Bill F McDonald*)

and went straight down, according to my wingman. I never had much confidence in the AIM-7!

'I was frustrated because Fred still didn't have a lock-on, and I couldn't see any missile out front. The MiG was continuing down in a shallow, banking turn to the right. I switched to "heat" and fired three AIM-9Es. The third ran up to the MiG and detonated.'

Both Col Wayne and Capt Profitt saw the aft section of the MiG burst into flames and begin to disintegrate. The pilot ejected.

'In my excitement I told *Red Parrot* to scratch one MiG-21!'

SECOND *LINEBACKER*

When *Linebacker I* ended on 22 October, in the hope that real negotiation with the North Vietnamese could begin, many of the TDY Phantom II units returned to their home bases. The 58th TFS (33rd TFW), the 307th TFS (31st TFW) and 523rd TFS (405th TFW) flew out of Udorn in late October. Korat lost the 35th TFS that same month when it returned to Kunsan AB, while the 469th TFS deactivated at the end of October.

At Udorn, one 'new' squadron did arrive towards the end of November 1972. *Rivet Haste* F-4Es with leading-edge slats, TISEO (Target Identification System, Electro-Optical), *Combat Tree* and the updated '556 Mod' cockpit were now becoming available. A batch of crews were given intensive air-to-air training on the improved F-4E by Mike Cooper and others, including 'real' dogfights with real *Have Drill* MiG-17s and *Have Donut* MiG-21s

A pair of 58th TFS F-4Es from Udorn top up during an October 1972 MiGCAP mission. Both carry full complements of AIM-7E and AIM-9J missiles, plus ALQ-101 (a 'long' ALQ-101(V)-3 on the F-4 to the right) and ALQ-87 ECM pods

For groundcrews at Udorn, working '24/7' meant getting a quick nap where and when you could while others kept the Phantom IIs flying (*Col Bill F McDonald*)

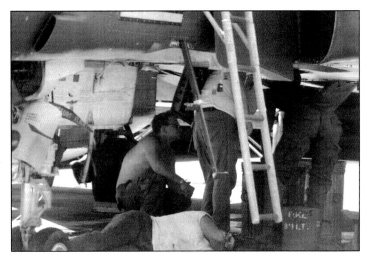

at Nellis AFB. This cadre then moved to Udorn as the 'New Nickel' 555th TFS to replace the personnel of the most successful, and experienced, fighter squadron in South-east Asia. In fact, they arrived just as *Linebacker I* finished, and therefore encountered no MiGs. Meanwhile, the 4th, 31st and 33rd TFWs continued to detach units to Udorn until September 1973.

It soon became clear that the North Vietnamese intended to continue their covert invasion of the South, rather than negotiate. President Nixon therefore decided to employ the sledgehammer of massive B-52 raids on the Hanoi/Haiphong areas to force a conclusion.

Operation *Linebacker II* began on 18 December 1972, and continued, day and night. F-4s and F-111As kept the MiGs' bases under constant attack, considerably reducing their sortie rates. The MiGs failed to down any B-52s, and as a last resort were told to ram the bombers if possible. Two VPAF pilots claimed B-52s before the attacks finished on 30 December, although the destruction of both bombers was attributed to SAMs by American analysts. A B-52 gunner claimed a MiG-21 on the night of 18 December, but the first F-4 kill of the new campaign did not happen until 22 December.

That day, Capt Gary Sholders and WSO 1Lt Eldon Binkley were leading 'Bucket' MiGCAP flight in a 'Triple Nickel' *Combat Tree* F-4D. They took up an orbit point after tanking, and shortly afterwards *Red Crown* vectored them towards a MiG west of Hanoi. The contact was below a thick cloudbank, and the F-4 crew chose to remain at their CAP station. When the bandit climbed to 16,000 ft, Sholders made a hard left and his WSO achieved radar contact with a target crossing to the left, 18 miles ahead of them. They rolled in behind the MiG, closing the gap to five miles and obtaining clearance to fire. At that point the MiG made a steep climb in afterburner and the F-4s followed, closing to three miles.

Binkley's radar then broke lock and they lost the target, reacquiring it shortly afterwards ten miles to the south. They pursued the contact but were unable to get a radar lock-on. *Red Crown* then told them that the MiG had turned onto a new heading, for Yen Bai airfield. Radar contact was made once again, this time at 25 miles. 'Bucket' flight closed to 20 miles from the MiG as it circled Yen Bai, but it was then warned not to land and headed off north-east, with the F-4 flight still in hot pursuit. Forty-six minutes after beginning the chase, and only seven miles from their prey, 'Bucket' had to break off at 'bingo' fuel levels and head home.

Three days later, intelligence sources established that a MiG-21 which had attempted a landing at Yen Bai on 21/22 December crashed soon afterwards with fuel starvation. Since 'Bucket' was the only USAF flight in the area following a MiG at that time, Capt Sholders and 1Lt Binkley were awarded a 'manoeuvring' kill.

Another 'Triple Nickel' F-4D crew added a MiG-21 to the

The 555th TFS sent this Christmas card to the VPAF in December 1972. As Ron Thurlow recalled, 'It bounced all around the world and eventually came back to the squadron'. He rescued it for posterity shortly afterwards (*Col R Thurlow*)

Lt Col Brunson stretches out in his F-4D front seat and Maj Stan Pickett looks relieved at the end of yet another 555th TFS mission in late 1972. Regularly crewing together during *Linebacker*, both men got a MiG-21 on 22 December 1972 (*Lt Col Ralph S Pickett*)

squadron's total the following day. Lt Col Jim Brunson piloted 66-0269 with WSO Maj Stan Pickett as 'Buick' leader on a strike escort mission in RP VI. The F-4D was one of six *Combat Tree* F-4Ds on squadron strength at the time, and as Stan Pickett remembered;

'The gear was working great that day. *Combat Tree*, totally operated from the back seat, was good for target range and azimuth, but it didn't help with altitude. We were allowed to tell *Disco* and *Red Crown* that we had an ID, without compromising security and letting the North Vietnamese know that *Combat Tree* could identify targets at such long range, but we could not fire if "friendlies" were in the forward fir-

An F-4D forms the backdrop for this group shot taken soon after the 22 December MiG kill by Jim Brunson and Stan Pickett (first and second from the left in the back row). Squatting at the extreme right is Capt Doug Hardgrave, who was among the first MiG killer WSOs in 1966. Having returned for another combat tour as a front-seater, he was Brunson's element leader on the MiG kill mission. His WSO, Doug Ochandarena, is standing immediately behind Hardgrave. The warning panel on the splitter plate refers to the F-4D's *Combat Tree* self-destruct device, but the other literature (visible in the front) is presumably aircrew instructional material (*via Doug Hardgrave*)

ing sector, which in this case they were. My timing was 40 seconds late due to an extra turn on the tanker, and I was concerned that the ingress CAP had already left. I knew the chaff flights were ahead of us since they were easy to see on radar. We were delayed by *Red Crown* for about ten seconds because of this. We actually fired our two missiles before clearance was given because it was a head-on shot, and the rapid closing rate was quickly taking away our advantage.

'We were the only flight protecting both the "chaffers" and the first group of B-52s. Our pact with the strikers was to protect them, and not go chasing MiGs, although this was not always adhered to. As "Buick 1", we were equipped with four AIM-7s, four AIM-9s, two ECM pods and three tanks. The centreline tank was jettisoned before firing AIM-7s, but we generally cleaned off all fuel tanks before a MiG engagement.

'Our time on station was usually ten to fifteen minutes, depending on how far north we flew and on the timing of the strike package. In fact, we

Christmas light relief. Lt Col Jim Brunson shakes hands with Bob Hope while Maj Stan Pickett accepts congratulations for their MiG kill. Hope flew more than two million miles for his many WSO shows, despite his professed hatred of flying (*USAF via Col R Thurlow*)

Like most F-4 squadrons in Southeast Asia, the bulk of the 308th TFS's work was bombing. F-4E-35-MC 67-0337 taxis out at Udorn with a full load of 16 Mk 82 500-lb bombs (*Col Bill F McDonald*)

had used so much fuel that day that we actually left before the next CAP moved onto station, although they were in the area.'

The CAP station was close to Kep airfield. *Red Crown* advised 'Buick' of two bandits, but Stan Pickett had already detected them;

'I was able to see the MiGs on the ground, preparing for take-off that day, but I could not get a radar target due to ground clutter. As soon as the MiGs climbed to altitude, I was able to pick them out at 27 miles, and actually had a lock-on at 23 miles. This was further away than we thought possible because of the small size of the MiG-21.'

As Jim Brunson pointed out, the F-4D's APQ-109 radar dish was larger than the APQ-120 in the F-4E, and 'was capable of longer-range contacts on smaller targets – if the radar was properly maintained. In combat, you never knew what you had for a radar until you were airborne!'

In Stan's case, the MiG was tracked flying left to right at a distance of 16 miles;

'It was obvious that they were heading for the "chaffers". I didn't realise until later that I was locked onto the lead MiG, who was not actually the "shooter". The trailing MiG was the "shooter", but it didn't matter because they could almost always cut and run if they were attacked by the CAP flight. However, from a professional viewpoint I would rather have shot the "shooter".'

Their MiG was 10,000 ft above 'Buick' flight when Brunson began his pull-up to fire at it. Four AIM-7E-2s were fired, as Stan Pickett recalled;

'Our confidence in the AIM-7 wasn't great, so most of us planned on firing all four as long as we were within parameters. We would have liked more opportunities to use the "Dogfight" Sparrow, but the rules of engagement for our missions didn't allow that chance.

'Our second missile hit the MiG in the tail section and the fourth passed through the same place. Our first missile was fired out of parameters but guided correctly, and the third was a dud that "cork-screwed" after firing. We didn't have a visual ID on the MiG until the missiles were already closing on it.'

The second MiG escaped as 'Buick' hit 'bingo' fuel and left the scene.

The final 'Triple Nickel' kill was also by an F-4D, much to the delight of the original 'Old Nickel' 555th TFS crews, and the chagrin of the 'New Nickel' *Rivet Haste* flyers, known at Udorn as 'grivets'. Stan Pickett remembered them well;

'We put them in a separate flight, since they had slatted F-4Es that required an instructional ride because of their different handling characteristics. We were so near the end of the war that new tactics were welcomed without resentment, although we did make fun of them by yelling "Grivet!" when they came into a briefing. They flew a spread formation – incorporating adapted Navy tactics – that allowed the

wingmen to search and lock. Whoever got the lock called it, and then became flight lead. The rest of the flight supported him and looked for enemy wingmen.

'By this time most crews were experienced, and this formation allowed for the best use of that experience and equipment. However, the results were mixed and inconclusive. The "grivets" never had enough credibility to take over the air-to-air mission.'

That last 555th TFS kill came during the evening of 28 December after a brief Christmas truce. Maj Harry McKee and Capt John Dubler were flying *Combat Tree* F-4D 66-7468 as 'List 1' on a MiGCAP 90 miles west of Hanoi. As Harry McKee remembered;

'The weather was clear, so my two-ship was in loose formation primarily so that we could watch out for other aircraft. The danger of mid-air collision was as real a threat as any other while almost 100 aircraft funnelled into North Vietnamese airspace from various refuelling tracks. Our running lights were on. In fact, my wingman Kim Rhine had his lights in "flash" mode.'

Red Crown vectored them onto a MiG-21 11 miles from their position, 'List' flight immediately initiating a ten-minute afterburner climb to 30,000 ft at a speed just 'over the Mach';

'Dragging three fuel tanks made that the best speed I could do. The MiG turned through west to a heading of 340 degrees, crossing my

Combat Tree **F-4D-29-MC 66-7468 carries a fresh MiG kill from its 28 December mission in which Maj Harry McKee and Capt John Dubler scored the penultimate MiG kill of the war** (*Don Jay via Peter Schinkelshoek*)

McKee and Dubler's MiG killer 66-7468 lines up for take-off as the war continues in the summer of 1973. Note that its OY codes have been lost prior to the jet transferring to another unit (*Col R Thurlow*)

Only one of the follow-on batch of 20 *Combat Tree* F-4Ds was lost in action, with the rest being reassigned to the 18th TFW at Kadena AB, on Okinawa, post-war. The two MiG kills marked on 66-0239, seen here landing at Udorn after a 1973 mission, may have been transferred from another aircraft as this was not a confirmed MiG killer (*Col R Thurlow*)

projected flight path at about ten miles. Its bright blue afterburner flame ended up creeping out at about "11 o'clock" as he progressed north.

'Since I was a re-treaded Air Defense Command navigator (from the Northrop F-89 Scorpion) who completed pilot training in 1963, the geometry of the two aircraft flight paths was easily visualised. We were not catching the MiG since he was going faster than us, at 1.4 Mach, but any intended targets, and his home base, were to the east (to our right). I assured John, "he has to turn east, and when he does we will shoot him down". I added, "If he doesn't go to China!"

'*Red Crown* cleared me to fire. "List 2" (Capt Kimzey Rhine and James Ogilvie) called "locked". As briefed, we were both ready to fire. Between two aircraft and four missiles, at least one good shot was likely. I reminded John to turn on the radar film camera. We were pretty excited. I told *Red Crown* we would be firing in about one minute, and asked them to tell another F-4 flight to our left that had a *Combat Tree* contact to stay clear. Forty-five seconds later the MiG pilot (Vu Xuan Thieu) started to turn right. Still on a heading of 010, climbing through 33,000 ft in the pitch dark of a moonless night, I let the radar-generated aiming dot drift from left to right as the MiG began to pass in front of us. Just as briefed, I squeezed my trigger while calling on the radio "'List 2', fire!"

'There was a blinding flash as my two missiles rippled off the aircraft and one came off Kim's. I didn't pick up my missile in flight for a few seconds as the motor flash had temporarily blinded me. I did get the impression that they barely wiggled from their course, which is not what you saw when you and the target were manoeuvring when you fired. Radar scope film showed the MiG slightly left of centre, and the aiming point was just two "mils" from dead centre.

'It seemed like only a second or two for the AIM-7E-2s to impact. I'm confident that Thieu saw them coming and tried to turn into them. The fireball was enormous, and all that came out of it was the burning, spinning MiG engine. The rest of the aircraft was virtually vaporised. Lt Col Curt Westphal saw the explosion from 150 miles away in the Udorn holding pattern. The missile impact came 57 seconds after my "one minute" call to *Red Crown*.

'It turned out that the first missile, that should have come off "List 2" had aborted, so mine got there first. I'm sorry Kim didn't get to share credit for the kill, since he did just what we had briefed.'

The final Vietnam MiG kill was also by a *Combat Tree* F-4D crew, although it took place after the *Linebacker II* onslaught, which ended on 29 December. Despite the halting of the offensive, F-4 crews were still allowed to tackle MiGs that threatened US air activity over the North.

On 8 January 1973, Capt Paul Howman (who had remained in-theatre after initially arriving with an 8th TFS/49th TFW TDY) and 1Lt Lawrence Kullman were leading 'Crafty' flight as an early morning MiGCAP in RP III, 80 miles south-west of Hanoi. Paul Howman described the ensuing MiG kill as 'a comedy of errors';

'The stan-eval folks said I needed a check flight so that I could lead flights over the following two weeks. My leader in the two-ship flight was my flight commander, but when taxying out he had to abort due to an aircraft problem. We had also launched an airborne spare F-4E, but his radar wasn't working. I joined up with him when we reached the pre-strike tanker. We had three two-ship flights that night as MiGCAPs for B-52s striking SAM sites around Vinh. One was led by the wing CO, Col Scott Smith, another by the 555th TFS CO (protecting the tankers) and then there was my flight in the middle.

Red Crown identified a MiG-21 65 miles north-east of them and vectored the F-4s to a position 26 nautical miles from the bandit;

'Since this was my first MiGCAP, I was trying to make the flight last as long as possible by "flying the bug" for maximum fuel endurance at 26,000 ft. Well, it looked like this was getting serious, so I raised the nose and tried to jettison the centreline tank. We had pulled the forward bay fairing circuit breaker to tell the aircraft we had no centreline tank so that we could monitor the status of the forward Sparrows instead. My centreline tank did not jettison, but I didn't know it. We had three fuel tanks, four AIM-7s and four AIM-9s. I decided to get low so as to have a better radar view upwards at the MiG. We had an 8000 ft undercast deck, and I wanted to get to about 10,000 ft, but almost overshot down to 8000 ft.

'*Red Crown* told us to turn to a heading of 300 degrees, but I only went to 330 so we could still look at the area where the MiG was. *Red Crown* caught us and told us to go to 300 degrees, which took the MiG off the radarscope. At the same time they vectored the wing commander's flight out to the east to fly up to the 19th parallel and do a double pincer movement with me.

'When we turned back on the MiG we had indications that it was out there but Larry Kullman couldn't find it. Then I saw its after-burner and put it in the centre of my windscreen, caged my radar straight ahead and got a lock-on. The radar locked, I shot (an AIM-7E-2) and remembered that you had to shoot two for the best probability of a kill. Both missiles came off, and Larry thought we had been hit because of the noise and flash of the Sparrows' motors. In fact, both forward

By the end of the war the 432nd TRW had amassed an impressive total of MiG kills, with 34 of its 36 victories resulting from engagements in 1972-73. MiG killer Harry McKee is seen here outside the wing HQ at Udorn (*Harry McKee*)

missiles hit the centreline tank as they launched, making two eight-inch long, half-inch deep scratches that could have knocked us out of the sky if the tanks had been penetrated and the fuel ignited.

'The first missile went as straight as an arrow, and I thought it might be a dud. The second did the classic AIM-7 barrel roll. Looking at the MiG's afterburner when the first missile detonated, I could see the delta shape of a MiG-21. The second missile looked as if it hit the MiG in the belly. There was a hesitation, and I thought it too might be a dud, but then the MiG blew up. The fuselage broke in half and the right wing came off. The wing CO radioed "Tally ho" on the burning wreckage. It fell through the 8000-ft undercast right in front of an F-111 on a strike mission.

'I then thought of the possibility of another MiG and turned towards the north where he came from. My wingman, without radar, had turned wider and was trying to get in position to fire a Sidewinder. At first I wasn't sure that he might not be a MiG, and we did a couple of scissors manoeuvres.

'Back at the tanker, my wingman informed me that I still had my centreline tank, so I filled it up as we still had another mission to fly – escorting a B-52 leaflet drop. My wingman returned to base with aircraft problems and I picked up an airborne spare at the tanker.'

Capt Howman completed his unpredictable mission by flying an approach to the wrong runway. Unknown to him, the designated runway had been changed, and he was thereby denied his original plan to perform an aileron roll before landing.

When bombing of the North ended and a cease-fire became effective on 29 January 1973, the total of four MiGs destroyed since the start of *Linebacker II* seemed surprisingly small. In fact, MiG opposition had been heavily suppressed by the persistent attacks on their airfields, command and control and logistics areas. Vietnamese sources suggest that only about 30 MiG-21s and 16 MiG-17s were operational in the latter part of 1972, and some of these were subsequently destroyed by bombing. Only about a dozen VPAF pilots were trained in night flying.

Although the MiG-21 pilots claimed several B-52s – the 'big prize' – Seventh Air Force attributed all losses to SAMs and admitted the loss of only one F-4E (67-0234) to a MiG at night. It was the last USAF aircraft to be hit by a VPAF fighter, and the only one to be shot down in a night-time battle. One other F-4E fell to a MiG while flying MiGCAP for the attempted rescue of an F-111A crew. This was 67-0292, a MiG killer for Lt Col Taft and Capt Imaye in July 1972.

During the *Linebacker* period the USAF had shot down 48 MiGs and lost 24 aircraft to MiGs – a neat 2-to-1 advantage. However, during the same period the US Navy's F-4 squadrons achieved a 6-to-1 ratio, shooting down 24 MiGs and losing only four of their own.

This disparity was widely attributed to the Navy's greater emphasis on air-to-air training through its Topgun programme, begun in 1968. USAF figures may also have been less favourable, as its fighters generally faced the MiG-21, whereas MiG-17s generally flew in areas where Navy strike packages were operating. Also, the Air Force strikes covered a larger area of terrain with longer ingress routes, allowing the VPAF more time to set its traps. Even so, the post-war years soon found the USAF setting up *Red Flag* – its own more elaborate version of Topgun.

APPENDICES

USAF F-4 PHANTOM II MiG KILLERS 1972-73

Date	MiG type	Type/Serial/Code	Sqn/Wing (of crew)	Crew	Callsign	Weapon
21/2/72	MiG-21	F-4D 65-0784/OY	555th TFS/432nd TRW	Maj R A Lodge/1Lt R C Locher	'Falcon 62'	AIM-7E
1/3/72	MiG-21	F-4D 66-7463/OY	555th TFS/432nd TRW	Lt Col J W Kittinger/1Lt L A Hodgdon	'Falcon 64'	AIM-7E
30/3/72	MiG-21	F-4D 66-0230/OC	13th TFS/432nd TRW	Capt F S Olmsted/Capt G R Volloy	'Papa 01'	AIM-7E
16/4/72	MiG-21	F-4D 66-7550/PN	13th TFS/432nd TRW	Maj E D Cherry/Capt J S Feinstein	'Basco 03'	AIM-7E
16/4/72	MiG-21	F-4D 66-7463/OY	13th TFS/432nd TRW	Capt F S Olmsted/ Capt S Maas	'Basco 01'	AIM-7E
16/4/72	MiG-21	F-4D 66-0280/PN	523rd TFS/432nd TRW	Capt J C Null/Capt M D Vahue	'Papa 03'	AIM-7E
8/5/72	MiG-19	F-4D 66-7463/OY	13th TFS/432nd TRW	Maj B P Crews/Capt K W Jones	'Galore 03'	AIM-7E
8/5/72	MiG-21	F-4D 65-0784/OY	555th TFS/432nd TRW	Maj R A Lodge/Capt R C Locher	'Oyster 01'	AIM-7E
10/5/72	MiG-21	F-4D 66-7463/OY	555th TFS/432nd TRW	Capt R S Ritchie/Capt C B DeBellevue	'Oyster 03'	AIM-7E
10/5/72	MiG-21	F-4D 65-0784/OY	555th TFS/432nd TRW	Maj R A Lodge/Capt R C Locher	'Oyster 01'	AIM-7E
10/5/72	MiG-21	F-4D 66-8734/OY	555th TFS/432nd TRW	1Lt J D Markle/Capt S D Eaves	'Oyster 02'	AIM-7E
11/5/72	MiG-21	F-4D 66-7661/PN	555th TFS/432nd TRW	Capt S E Nichols/1Lt J R Bell	'Gopher 02'	AIM-7E
12/5/72	MiG-19	F-4D 66-8756/OY	555th TFS/432nd TRW	Lt Col W T Frye/Lt Col J P Cooney	'Harlow 02'	AIM-7E
23/5/72	MiG-19	F-4E 67-0333/LC	35th TFS/366th TFW	Lt Col L L Beckers/Capt J F Huwe	'Balter 01'	AIM-7E
23/5/72	MiG-21	F-4E 67-0333/LC	35th TFS/366th TFW	Capt J M Beatty/Capt J M Sumner	'Balter 02'	M61A-1
31/5/72	MiG-21	F-4E 68-0338/ED	13th TFS/432nd TRW	Capt B G Leonard/Capt J S Feinstein	'Gopher 03'	AIM-9E
31/5/72	MiG-21	F-4D 65-0801/OC	555th TFS/432nd TRW	Capt R S Ritchie/Capt L H Pettit	'Icebag 01'	AIM-7E
2/6/72	MiG-19	F-4E 67-0210/ZF	58th TFS/432nd TRW	Maj P W Handley/1Lt J J Smallwood	'Brenda 01'	M61A-1
21/6/72	MiG-21	F-4E 67-0283/JV	469th TFS/388th TFW	Lt Col V R Christiansen/Maj K M Harden	'Iceman 03'	AIM-9E
8/7/72	MiG-21	F-4E 67-0362/ED	555th TFS/432nd TRW	Capt R S Ritchie/Capt C B DeBellevue	'Paula 01'	AIM-7E-2
8/7/72	MiG-21	F-4E 67-0362/ED	555th TFS/432nd TRW	Capt R S Ritchie/Capt C B DeBellevue	'Paula 01'	AIM-7E-2
18/7/72	MiG-21	F-4D 66-0271/OC	13th TFS/432nd TRW	Lt Col C G Baily/Capt J S Feinstein	'Snug 01'	AIM-9E
29/7/72	MiG-21	F-4E 67-0292/LA	4th TFS/366th TFW	Lt Col T E Taft/Capt S M Imaye	'Pistol 01'	AIM-7E-2
29/7/72	MiG-21	F-4D 66-0271/OC	13th TFS/432nd TRW	Lt Col C G Baily/Capt J S Feinstein	'Cadillac 01'	AIM-7E-2
12/8/72	MiG-21	F-4E 67-0239/ZF	58th TFS/432nd TRW	Capt L G Richard (USMC)/Lt Cdr M J Ettell (US Navy)	'Dodge 01'	AIM-7E-2
15/8/72	MiG-21	F-4E 69-7235/SC	336th TFS/8th TFW	Capt F W Sheffler/Capt M A Massen	'Date 04'	AIM-7E-2
19/8/72	MiG-21	F-4E 69-0291/LA	4th TFS/366th TFW	Capt S E White/Capt F E Bettine	'Pistol 03'	AIM-7E-2
28/8/72	MiG-21	F-4D 66-7463/OY	555th TFS/432nd TRW	Capt R S Ritchie/ Capt C B DeBellevue	'Buick 01'	AIM-7E-2
2/9/72	MiG-19	F-4E 67-0392/JV	34th/35th TFS/388th TFW	Maj J I Lucas/1Lt D G Malloy	'Eagle 03'	AIM-7E-2
9/9/72	MiG-21	F-4E 67-0327/ZF	555th TFS/432nd TRW	Capt C B Tibbett/1Lt W S Hargrove	'Olds 03'	M61A-1
9/9/72	MiG-19	F-4D 66-0267/OY	555th TFS/432nd TRW	Capt J A Madden/Capt C B DeBellevue	'Olds 01'	AIM-9J
9/9/72	MiG-19	F-4D 66-0267/OY	555th TFS/432nd TRW	Capt J A Madden/Capt C B DeBellevue	'Olds 01'	AIM-9J
12/9/72	MiG-21	F-4E 67-0275/JJ	35th TFS/388th TFW	Lt Col L L Beckers/1Lt T M Griffin	'Finch 01'	AIM-9E/M61A-1
12/9/72	MiG-21	F-4E 67-0268/JJ	35th TFS/388th TFW	Maj G L Retterbush/1Lt D L Autrey	'Finch 03'	M61A-1
12/9/72	MiG-21	F-4D 65-0608/UP	469th TFS/388 TFW	Capt M J Mahaffey/1Lt G I Shields	'Robin 02'	AIM-9E
16/9/72	MiG-21	F-4E 68-0338/ED	555th TFS/432nd TRW	Capt C B Tibbett/1Lt W S Hargrove	'Chevy 03'	AIM-9J
5/10/72	MiG-21	F-4E 68-0493/JJ	34th TFS/388th TFW	Capt R E Coe/1Lt O E Webb	'Robin 01'	AIM-7E-2
6/10/72	MiG-19	F-4E 67-0392/JV	34th TFS/388th TFW	Maj G L Clouser/1Lt C H Brunson	'Eagle 03'	Manoeuvring with 66-0313
6/10/72	MiG-19	F-4E 66-0313/JV	34th TFS/388th TFW	Capt C D Barton/1Lt G D Watson	'Eagle 04'	Manoeuvring with 67-0392
8/10/72	MiG-21	F-4E 69-0276/JJ	35th TFS/388th TFW	Maj G L Retterbush/Capt R H Jasperson	'Lark 01'	M61A-1
12/10/72	MiG-21	F-4D 66-0268/OY	555th TFS/432nd TRW	Capt J A Madden/Capt L H Pettit	'Vega 01'	Manoeuvring
13/10/72	MiG-21	F-4D 66-7501/OC	13th TFS/432nd TRW	Lt Col C D Westphal/Capt J S Feinstein	'Olds 01'	AIM-7E-2
15/10/72	MiG-21	F-4E 67-0301/JJ	34th TFS/388th TFW	Maj R L Holtz/1Lt W C Diehl	'Parrot 03'	AIM-9E
15/10/72	MiG-21	F-4E 67-0232/ZF	307th TFS/432nd TRW	Capt G M Rubus/Capt J L Hendrickson	'Buick 03'	M61A-1
15/10/72	MiG-21	F-4D 66-7463/OY	523rd TFS/432nd TRW	Maj I J McCoy/Maj F W Brown	'Chevy 01'	AIM-9E
21/12/72	MiG-21	F-4D 66-0240/OY	555th TFS/432nd TRW	Capt G L Sholders/1Lt E D Binkley	'Bucket 01'	Manoeuvring
22/12/72	MiG-21	F-4D 66-0269/OY	555th TFS/432nd TRW	Lt Col J E Brunson/Maj R S Pickett	'Buick 01'	AIM-7E-2
28/12/72	MiG-21	F-4D 66-7468/OY	555th TFS/432nd TRW	Maj H L McKee /Capt J E Dubler	'List 01'	AIM-7E-2
7/1/73	MiG-21	F-4D 65-0796/??*	4th TFS/432nd TRW	Capt P D Howman/1Lt L W Kullman	'Crafty 01'	AIM-7E-2

* this aircraft may possibly have been uncoded at the time of its MiG kill, ready for transfer to another unit

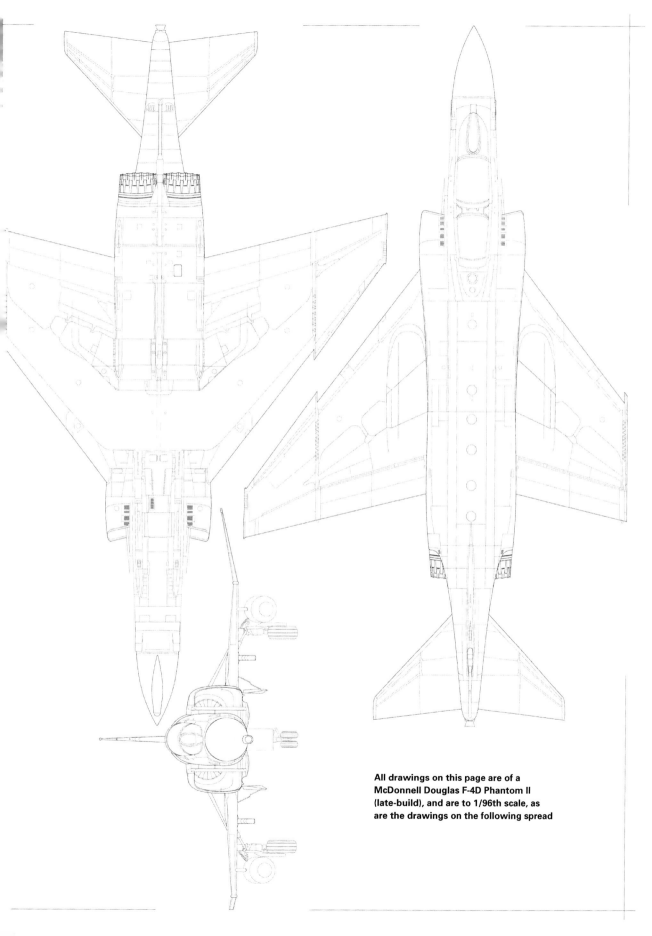

**All drawings on this page are of a
McDonnell Douglas F-4D Phantom II
(late-build), and are to 1/96th scale, as
are the drawings on the following spread**

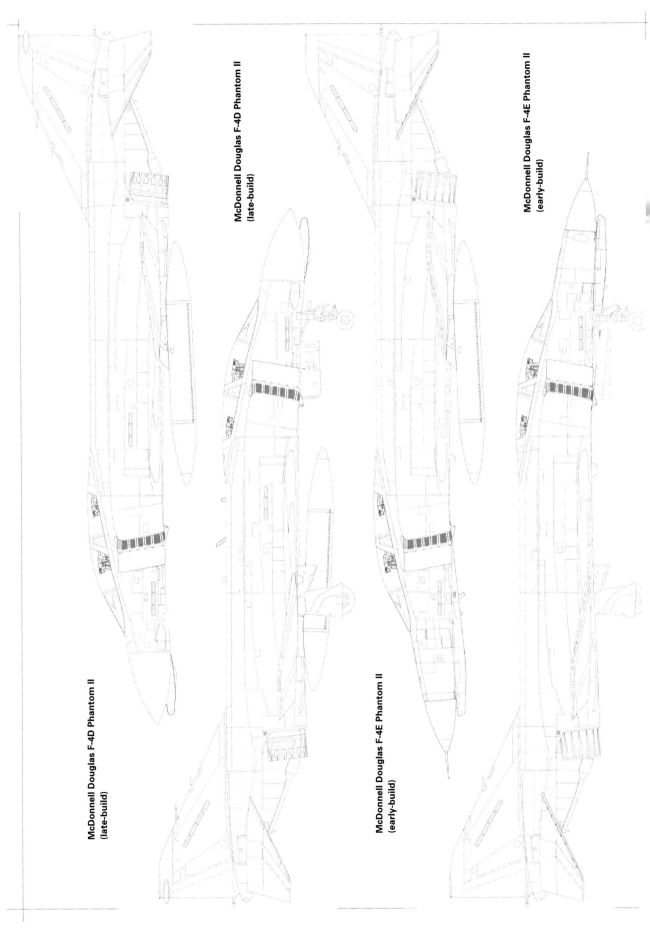

**McDonnell Douglas F-4D Phantom II
(late-build)**

**McDonnell Douglas F-4D Phantom II
(late-build)**

**McDonnell Douglas F-4E Phantom II
(early-build)**

**McDonnell Douglas F-4E Phantom II
(early-build)**

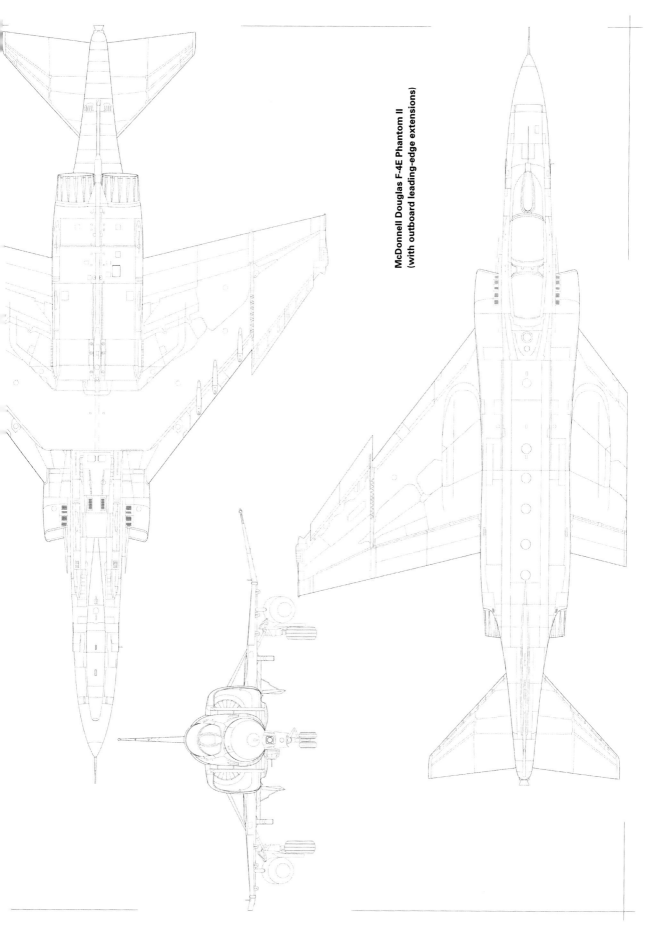

McDonnell Douglas F-4E Phantom II
(with outboard leading-edge extensions)

1
F-4D-29-MC 65-0784 of Maj R A Lodge and Capt R C Locher, 555th TFS/432nd TRW, Udorn RTAB, 21 February 1972

This aircraft was delivered to the USAF on 23 November 1966. It initially served with the 479th TFW's 4535th CCTS (GA codes) at George AFB, California. On 15 January 1970 the jet was reassigned to the 475th TFW's 391st TFS (UD) at Misawa AB. The latter unit's aircraft, and its codes, were transferred to the 80th TFS/3rd TFW at Kunsan AB, South Korea, on 15 March 1971, and this F-4D joined the unit nine days later. It then flew with the 555th TFS from 4 January 1972 until it was shot down on 10 May 1972 by a MiG-19 just minutes after Lodge and Locher had achieved their third MiG kill with the fighter. Although WSO Locher ejected, Lodge remained aboard the stricken jet and was killed when it crashed. Becoming a pilot post-war, Locher later commanded the 4453rd TES, testing the F-117A.

2
F-4D-29-MC 66-0230 of Capt F S Olmsted Jr and Capt G R Volloy, 13th TFS/432nd TRW, Udorn RTAB, 30 March 1972

Used by Capt F S Olmsted Jr and Capt G R Volloy for their MiG-21 kill on 30 March 1972 during Olmsted's 300th mission, this aircraft was delivered new to the 479th TFW's 4535th CCTS on 29 December 1966. Like 65-0784 (profile 1), it was transferred to the 475th TFW's 391st TFS on 15 January 1970. The jet also moved to the 80th TFS/3rd TFW on 24 March, and subsequently joined the 432nd TRW on 17 December 1971. Assigned to the wing's 13th TFS (OC), this *Combat Tree* F-4D was downed on 11 May 1972 by an 'Atoll' missile fired by a 927th FR MiG-21 flown by Ngo Van Phu.

3
F-4D-31-MC 66-7550 of Maj E D Cherry and Capt J S Feinstein, 13th TFS/432nd TRW, Udorn RTAB, 16 April 1972

This F-4 was delivered new to the 15th TFW at MacDill AFB, Florida, on 23 March 1967. Passed on to the 4th TFW's 334th TFS (SA) at Seymour Johnson AFB, North Carolina, on 26 January 1968, the aircraft joined the 432nd TRW at Udorn on 18 June 1970. It moved again on 19 May 1971 when the fighter was transferred to the 405th TFW's 523rd TFS (PN) at Clark AB, the Philippines, on 19 May 1971. Service with the 36th TFS/3rd TFW (and a code change from UK to UP) followed until 28 June 1974. Three months later, on 16 September, the jet was reassigned to the 8th TFW (WP) at Kunsan, and it received Maverick capability in 1976. The F-4 moved to the 51st TFW (OS) at Osan AB, South Korea, on 1 January 1982, but it returned to the 8th TFW on 28 June 1982. The jet was issued to the USAF Reserve (AFRES) on 21 December 1982, flying with the 507th FG's 465th TFS (SH) at Tinker AFB, Oklahoma, and subsequently the 906th TFG's 89th TFS (DO) at Wright-Patterson AFB, Ohio, from May 1989. The veteran F-4 was put on permanent display at VFW Post 8437 in Enon, Ohio, on 19 October 1991, having first been displayed at Tinker AFB.

4
F-4D-29-MC 66-0280 of Capt J C Null and Capt M D Vahue, 523rd TFS/432nd TRW, Udorn RTAB, 16 April 1972

66-0280 was delivered new to the 479th TFW on 29 January 1967. It then moved to the 33rd TFW's 4533rd TTS (EG) at Eglin AFB, Florida, on 27 February 1969. Reassigned to PACAF less than two months later, the jet joined the 405th TFW's 523rd TFS on 8 April 1969. It was then reassigned to the 3rd TFW's 36th TFS (UK) on 11 November 1972. Re-coded UP on 27 October 1973, the Phantom II came under 8th TFW control on 16 September 1974. Just under four weeks later, on 11 October, the F-4 was transferred to the 48th TFW (LN) at RAF Lakenheath, in England. The fighter returned to the US on 5 April 1977 and joined the 474th TFW (NA) at Nellis AFB, Nevada, as part of Operation *Ready Switch*. Reissued to the Homestead-based 31st TFW (ZF) on 16 April 1980, 66-0280 joined the Texas ANG's 111th FIS/147th FIG at Ellington ANGS on 15 March 1987. Withdrawn from use two years later, the jet was placed on display at Ellington in December 1989.

5
F-4D-32-MC 66-8734 of 1Lt J D Markle and Capt S D Eaves, 555th TFS/432nd TRW, Udorn RTAB, 10 May 1972

This jet was delivered new to the Ogden Air Materiel Area (AMA) on 14 October 1967. Subsequently issued to the 8th TFW on 20 November 1967, it was reassigned to the 405th TFW's 523rd TFS (PN) just ten days later. Returned to Ogden AMA on 30 January 1971, the F-4 received *Pave Phantom* (LORAN) equipment on site and was then reassigned to the 432nd TRW's 555th TFS (OY). Having seen much combat in 1971-73, the aircraft went on to serve with the 48th TFW (LN) from 2 August 1974 and then the 52nd TFW (SP) at Spangdahlem AB, Germany, from 21 January 1975. Its final USAF service was with the AFRES's 301st TFW's 457th TFS (TH) at Carswell AFB, Texas, from 1 April 1982. By then it had received ASQ-153 *Pave Spike* TV/LGB capability. 66-8734 was one of 24 F-4Ds supplied to the Republic of Korea Air Force (RoKAF) between December 1987 and April 1988, and it is almost certainly still flying in frontline service today.

6
F-4D-29-MC 66-7463 of Capt R S Ritchie and Capt C B DeBellevue, 555th TFS/432nd TRW, Udorn RTAB, 10 May 1972

66-7463 was used by future aces Capts R S Ritchie

and C B DeBellevue to claim their MiG-21 kill on 10 May 1972, this victory being the fourth credited to the aircraft. Delivered new on 28 January 1967 to the 479th TFW, this *Combat Tree* F-4D was passed on to the recently formed 57th FWW's 414th FWS (WD) at Nellis AFB on 19 November 1969. It was reassigned to the 479th TFW just over a month later, before being transferred to the 475th TFW at Misawa AB, Japan, on 11 January 1970. Here, the F-4 spent time with both the 391st (UD) and 67th TFSs (UP). The latter codes were retained for its service with the 35th TFS/3rd TFW from 24 March 1971, and on 4 January 1972 the aircraft began its spectacular combat career with the 432nd TRW. Having survived the war with six kills to its credit, the fighter was reassigned to the 8th TFW on 16 January 1974, before reverting back to 432nd TRW control on 15 June that same year. The jet was issued to the 18th TFW (ZZ) at Kadena AB, on Okinawa, on 27 June 1975. Five years later, on 3 May 1980, it joined the 31st TFW/TTW (ZF) at Homestead AFB. Finally retired from active service in October 1986, the F-4 was subsequently placed on permanent display in the grounds of the USAF Academy in Colorado Springs. In this profile, the Phantom II has been adorned with MiG kills for Kittinger/Hodgdon (large star), Olmsted/Maas (second largest star) and Crews/Jones (star at bottom left).

7

F-4E-35-MC 67-0333 of Capt J M Beatty and 1Lt J M Sumner, 35th TFS/366th TFW, Da Nang AB, 23 May 1972

This jet was delivered to the USAF on 9 November 1968 and issued to the 33rd TFW 26 days later. Having seen combat on TDY with the 366th TFW in 1971-72, the jet was permanently transferred to PACAF's 432nd TRW on 29 October 1972. On 24 June 1974, the fighter switched to the 3rd TFW's 36th TFS (UK), and it briefly remained with the wing after it was re-designated the 8th TFW on 16 September that same year. Staying in PACAF, 67-0333's next assignment was with the 51st CW (OS) from 30 September 1974. It received Leading Edge Slats (LES) in April 1975. Service with the 3rd TFW (PN) followed from 20 August 1977, and then the 35th TFW/TTW (GA) from 20 July 1979 to 11 October 1989. Relegated to the Aerospace Maintenance And Regeneration Center (AMARC) at Davis-Monthan AFB, Arizona, on 11 October 1989, the jet was exported to Bodo, Norway, for static display on 1 August 1997.

8

F-4E-33-MC 67-0210 of Maj P W Handley and 1Lt J J Smallwood, 58th TFS/432nd TRW, Udorn RTAB, 2 June 1972

This F-4E was delivered new to the 33rd TFW's 4533rd TTS on 9 July 1968. It was reassigned to the 4531st TFW (ZF) at Homestead AFB on 13 August 1970, the wing being re-designated the 31st TFW (ZF) on 15 October 1970. Like most surviving USAF F-4Es, this aircraft received LES updates in 1974. Six years later, in August 1980, the jet finally moved to the 4th TFW (SJ), with whom it remained until being retired to AMARC on 18 September 1986. There were plans to recover the aircraft for display, but it was sold to Turkey in June 1987 before this could be done. Most recently serving with Konya-based 132 *Filo*, 67-0210 was withdrawn from use in October 2004.

9

F-4E-35-MC 67-0283 of Lt Col V R Christiansen and Maj K M Harden, 469th TFS/388th TFW, Korat RTAB, 21 June 1972

This aircraft claimed the 388th TFW's first MiG kill when Lt Col V R Christiansen and Maj K M Harden destroyed a MiG-21 kill on 21 June 1972. Accepted by the USAF from McDonnell Douglas on 29 August 1968, it was issued to the 33rd TFW on 11 October 1968. The fighter was then delivered to the 388th TFW, where it served with the 469th (JV) and 34th TFSs (JJ). Reassigned to the 432nd TRW on 29 June 1974, the jet was one of 304 early-build F-4Es to received LES updates, its rework taking place in October 1975. Use by the 3rd TFW then followed (from 12 December 1975 to 20 January 1977), after which it served with the 21st CW (FC) at Elmendorf AFB, Alaska, until April 1981. The jet joined the 4th TFW in October 1982, with whom it remained until September 1985 when it became one of 40 F-4Es supplied to the RoKAF.

10

F-4E-34-MC 67-0270 of Capt R F Hardy and Capt P T Lewinski, 4th TFS/366th TFW, Takhli RTAB, 8 July 1972

This aircraft was delivered new to the 33rd TFW on 9 August 1968. It moved to PACAF on 10 May 1969 when it joined the 388th TFW's 34th TFS (JJ) at Korat RTAB. The F-4 then transferred to the 4th TFS/366th TFW at Da Nang AB on 4 December 1969. The 4th TFS came under 432nd TRW control on 29 October 1972. Returning to the USA in January 1973, the jet served with the 4th TFW for the next six months. Updated with LES, it was transferred to the 57th FWW (WA) on 26 November 1973, and then joined the 31st TFW in October 1979. Withdrawn from use in November 1990, 67-0270 was placed on permanent display at McGuire AFB, New Jersey, in March 1994.

11

F-4E-36-MC 67-0362 of Capt R S Ritchie and Capt C B DeBellevue, 58th TFS/432nd TRW, Udorn RTAB, 8 July 1972

This F-4E first flew on 1 October 1968 and was delivered to the 479th TFW's 434th TFS (GD) on 12 February 1969. It was reassigned to the 33rd TFW's 16th TFS on 17 April 1970 – the unit was re-designated the 58th TFS on 1 November 1970. The jet remained here until 19 October 1973, when it became one of 34 *Nickel Grass* F-4Es hastily supplied to the Israeli Defense Force/Air Force (IDF/AF). All Israeli F-4s were retired in May 2004.

12

F-4E-34-MC 67-0292 of Lt Col T E Taft and Capt S M Imaye, 4th TFS/366th TFW, Takhli RTAB, 29 July 1972

Delivered new to the 33rd TFW on 22 October 1968, this aircraft was transferred to PACAF to serve with the 366th TFW's 4th TFS (LA) on 9 April 1969. Sustaining battle damage in August 1972, the jet was repaired by Air Asia and reassigned to the 13th TFS/432nd TRW. It was the first of two F-4Es shot down by MiG-21 pilot Tran Viet of the 921st FR on 27 December 1972. 67-0292's crew, pilot Maj C H Jeffcoat and WSO 1Lt J R Trimble, were flying a MiGCAP during a search and rescue effort for a downed F-111A crew at the time. Both men became PoWs.

13

F-4E-43-MC 69-7235 of Capt F W Sheffler and Capt M A Massen, 336th TFS/8th TFW, Ubon RTAB, 19 August 1972

Delivered new to the 4th TFW on 16 October 1970, this jet served with the 336th TFS (initially SC codes, but re-coded SJ by December 1972) prior to being reassigned to the 31st TFW (ZF) on 17 December 1973. Transferred to the 33rd TFW's 58th TFS (ED) on 6 June 1974, it had LES updates in mid-1975 and was then issued to the 347th TFW (MY) at Moody AFB, Georgia, on 1 December 1975. The fighter remained here until 3 August 1978, when it was withdrawn from service and converted into an F-4G Wild Weasel. The aircraft was subsequently sent to the 35th TFW (WW) at George AFB on 5 February 1979, and it remained with the unit until the 37th TFW (WW) took control of the 35th's F-4Gs on 30 March 1981. In December 1982 the aircraft joined the 4485th TS/TAWC at Eglin AFB, before moving to the 57th FW's 422nd TES (WA) on 21 January 1993. The F-4 ended its frontline career with the wing on 30 November 1995. Following a period in storage at AMARC, the weary jet was converted into a QF-4G target drone in May 1996. Lt Col Bob Kay, commander of the 82nd ATRS's Det 1, reported to its former pilot, MiG killer Fred Sheffler, 'Your jet died a glorious death on 5 May 1998 over the Gulf Range in Florida. It took an AIM-120 AMRAAM "in the face" from an F-16. It's been a tough job watching these old warriors die, but better they go this way in a blaze of glory than rotting in the desert'.

14

F-4E-42-MC 69-0291 of Capt S E White and Capt F E Bettine, 4th TFS/366th TFW, Takhli RTAB, 19 August 1972

Delivered new to the 4th TFW's 336th TFS on 9 July 1970, this fighter joined the 366th TFW (LA) on 27 July 1972 – this unit came under 432nd TRW control from 31 October 1972. The jet received the LES modification in May 1974, and then returned to the 432nd TRW (re-designated the 3rd TFW in December 1975). Transferred to the 21st CW on 9 November 1979, the F-4 subsequently served with the 35th TFW from November 1982, the 347th TFW

from March 1984 and the 51st TFW from April 1988. Returning to the 3rd TFW (PN) in April 1990, the aircraft was retired seven months later and put on display at Osan AB, South Korea.

15

F-4D-29-MC 66-7463 of Capt R S Ritchie and Capt C B DeBellevue, 555th TFS/432nd TRW, Udorn RTAB, 28 August 1972

This aircraft was used by Capts R S Ritchie and C B DeBellevue for their MiG-21 kill on 28 August 1972. This victory gave Ritchie his all important fifth kill, making him the USAF's first F-4 ace. Note the application of electro-luminescent formation lights to 66-7463. The jet carried four MiG kills on its splitter plate during the action, and a fifth was added upon its return to Udorn. Crew names, including crew chief Sgt Reginald Taylor, were stencilled on the jet's nose.

16

F-4D-29-MC 66-0267 of Capt J A Madden and Capt C B DeBellevue, 555th TFS/432nd TRW, Udorn RTAB, 9 September 1972

This *Combat Tree* F-4D was delivered new to the 479th TFW on 25 January 1967. It moved to the 49th TFW at Holloman AFB, New Mexico, on 27 December 1968, and then onto the 4th TFW on 16 January 1969. Reassigned to PACAF, the fighter was taken on charge by the 8th TFW at Ubon RTAB on 5 December 1969. It then transferred to the 432nd TRW on 2 November 1970, before joining the 405th FW's 523rd TFS (PN) at Clark AB on 5 June 1971. The F-4 remained with this unit until 20 August 1972 when it returned to the 432nd TRW. The aircraft was then reassigned to the 18th TFW on 7 July 1975, with whom it served until flown to Ogden ALC on 21 June 1979. The fighter's final assignment was to the 31st TFW/TTW (ZF, and later HS codes), with whom it flew from 27 November 1979 through to 13 March 1985. It has been on static display at Homestead AFB since 21 March 1988.

17

F-4E-34-MC 67-0268 of Maj G L Retterbush and 1Lt D L Autrey, 469th TFS/388th TFW, Korat RTAB, 12 September 1972

Delivered new to the 33rd TFW on 11 July 1968, this aircraft was transferred to PACAF for assignment to the 388th TFW on 17 November 1968. It served with the wing's 469th TFS (JV) until the squadron disestablished on 31 October 1972, when it switched to the 34th TFS (JJ). The fighter was then passed on to the 3rd TFW's 36th TFS (UK) on 17 August 1974 after LES modification. Further PACAF service with the 51st CW followed from 30 September 1974 until November 1982, when the jet joined the 21st CW/TFW. Its final USAF service was with the 37th TFW, with whom it flew from October 1985 through to 27 July 1987, when it was supplied to the Turkish Air Force. 67-0268 is still presently in frontline service with 131 *Filo* at Konya air base.

18

F-4E-37-MC 68-0338 of Capt C B Tibbett and 1Lt W S Hargrove, 555th TFS/432nd TRW, Udorn RTAB, 16 September 1972

A dual MiG-21 killer, this F-4E was delivered new to the 4531st TFW's 478th TFS (ZE) on 14 March 1969. It moved to the 33rd TFW's 16th TFS (ED) on 20 May 1970, before switching to the wing's 58th TFS (ED). Brief service with the 4th TFW followed between 9 October and 17 December 1972, after which it joined the 31st TFW (ZF). Remaining here until 6 June 1973, the combat veteran then returned to the 58th TFS/33rd TFW – it received the LES modification during its second spell with the Eglin-based wing. The fighter rejoined the 31st TFW on 24 April 1978, after which it was reassigned to the 21st CW/TFW from 8 June 1979 to January 1982. The F-4 then spent the next two years with the 35th TFW, prior to finishing off its frontline career with the 57th FWW. In September 1985 the aircraft joined the Missouri ANG's 110th TFS/131st TFW (SL), and it served with the wing until being retired in 1991. It has been on permanent display at Lambert St Louis International Airport, Missouri, since October 1996.

19

F-4E-40-MC 68-0493 of Capt R E Coe and 1Lt O E Webb, 34th TFS/388th TFW, Korat RTAB, 5 October 1972

This aircraft was delivered new to the 479th TFW on 12 December 1969, serving with the wing's 434th TFS (GD). It was passed to the 21st CW's 43rd TFS on 9 September 1970, where it remained until 15 August 1972. After a month with the 366th TFW, the jet was reassigned to the 388th TFW's 34th TFS from 20 September to 1 November 1972, when the aircraft came under 432nd TRW control. It returned to the 21st CW on 12 January 1973, and remained with the wing until November 1976 – the F-4 had received LES updates by July 1974. Issued to the 3rd TFW in late 1976, the fighter had completed almost a decade of service with the Philippines-based wing by the time it was sold to the RoKAF in June 1986.

20

F-4E-36-MC 67-0392 of Maj G L Clouser and 1Lt C H Brunson, 469th TFS/388th TFW, Korat RTAB, 6 October 1972

A dual MiG-19 killer, 67-0392 was delivered to the 479th TFW on 5 March 1969 and reassigned to the 388th TFW on 30 August 1970 – it flew primarily with the 469th TFS during its time with the wing. The jet then served with the 432nd TRW between 8 October 1972 and 31 January 1973, after which it moved to the 58th TFS/33rd TFW. It remained here until 4 November 1974, when the fighter joined the 1st TFW (FF) at MacDill AFB, Florida. A period with the co-located 56th TFW (MC) followed from 30 June 1975 (during which time it received its LES modification) until the F-4 was reassigned to the 33rd TFW two years later. On 3 April 1979 the fighter moved to the 4th TFW, then joined the

347th TFW on 29 June 1979 and finally the AFRES's 457th TFS/301st TFW from 12 November 1987. It served with the reserves until its retirement on 22 October 1990. The jet has been on display within the Virginia Air and Space Center in Hampton, Virginia, since the museum's opening in 1992. Indeed, due to its size it had to be in place inside the new facility before the west wall of the Center could be completed in late 1991!

21

F-4E-32-MC 66-0313 of Capt C D Barton and 1Lt G D Watson, 34th TFS/388th TFW, Korat RTAB, 6 October 1972

Delivered new to the 33rd TFW on 30 January 1968, this aircraft was passed onto the 15th TFW on 27 September 1968 and the 4530th TTS/1st TFW on 1 October 1970. Service with the 388th TFW, including the 469th TFS (JV), followed from 28 January 1971. The aircraft came under 432nd TRW control from 8 October to 8 December 1972, when it was reassigned to the 58th TFS/33rd TFW, remaining with that wing until 19 October 1973. It was included in a batch of 34 *Nickel Grass* transfers to the IDF/AF later that year. Serving as Kurnass (Hebrew for 'heavy hammer') 331 in Israeli service the aircraft ended its frontline career in the late 1990s and was supplied to the Holtz Technical High School (a branch of the IDF/AF Technical College) in Tel Aviv. In 2004 the aircraft was relocated to Ramon air base, in the Negev Desert, for preservation as a gate guard.

22

F-4E-42-MC 69-276 of Maj G L Retterbush and Capt R H Jasperson, 34th TFS/388th TFW, Korat RTAB, 8 October 1972

Delivered new to the 4th TFW's 336th TFS on 17 July 1970, this aircraft was reassigned to the 34th TFS on 1 January 1972. The fighter was downed with an 'Atoll' by MiG-21 ace Nguyen Duc Soat on 12 October 1972, Capt Joe Young and MiG-killer 1Lt Cecil Brunson, being taken prisoner.

23

F-4D-29-MC 66-7463 of Maj I J McCoy and Maj F W Brown, 555th TFS/432nd TRW, Udorn RTAB 15 October 1972

66-7463 achieved its sixth, and final, MiG-21 kill on 15 October 1972, with Majs I J McCoy and F W Brown from the 523rd TFS at the controls. The jet was marked with five MiG kill stars, each with 'MiG-21' stencilled within it, on its port splitter plate during this mission. The F-4 was later repainted with several different six-star patterns.

24

F-4E-35-MC 67-0301 of Maj R L Holtz and 1Lt W C Diehl, 34th TFS/388th TFW, Korat RTAB, 15 October 1972

This aircraft was used by Maj R L Holtz and 1Lt W C Diehl for their MiG-21 kill on 15 October 1972, which proved to be the last for the 388th TFW. This jet's long service career began with the 33rd TFW on 2 August 1968. It was transferred to the 388th TFW on 17 November that same year, flying with the 469th and then the 34th TFSs. It remained with the latter unit after it came under 432nd TRW control, finally leaving the 34th on 7 September 1975, having had its LES updates. Following Programmed Depot Maintenance (PDM) in the US, it was reassigned to the 21st CW on 12 December 1975, then the 35th TFW/TTW from 27 July 1979. The jet remained with the latter wing until it was supplied to the Turkish Air Force in 1992 as 'payment' for the country's support in the Gulf War of the previous year – the Turks received 40 surplus F-4Es as part of the deal. Flown by 112 *Filo* from Eskisehir, this aircraft was one of two Turkish Phantom IIs to violate Greek airspace near Athens on the afternoon of 28 December 1995. Two Greek Air Force F-16s that were scrambled to intercept them caught up with the F-4s as they headed east for Turkish airspace. Both pilots then saw 67-0301 crash into Greek territorial waters near the island of Lesbos following an apparent mechanical failure. The WSO, who ejected, was rescued by a Greek helicopter, but the pilot was never found.

25
F-4E-34-MC 67-0232 of Capt G M Rubus and Capt J L Hendrickson, 307th TFS/432nd TRW, Udorn RTAB, 15 October 1972
Delivered to the 15th TFW's 46th TFS (FD) at MacDill AFB on 12 June 1968, 67-0232 served with this unit until being reassigned to the 4531st TFW's 560th TFS on 21 January 1970. The wing was re-designated the 31st TFW on 15 October 1970, and the F-4E remained with the outfit at Homestead AFB until May 1980 – it received LES during a PDM in August 1974. The jet joined the 4th TFW after leaving the 31st, and on completion of its service at Seymour Johnson it was stored at AMARC from September 1986 to June 1987. The F-4 was then flown to Ogden Air Logistics Center (ALC) for refurbishment, after which it was supplied to the Turkish Air Force on 13 October 1987. Initially issued to 131 *Filo*, the aircraft is presently serving with 132 *Filo* at Konya.

26
F-4D-29-MC 66-0269 of Lt Col J E Brown and Maj R S Pickett, 13th TFS/432nd TRW, Udorn RTAB, 22 December 1972
This *Combat Tree* F-4D was initially delivered new to USAFE's 417th TFS (HA)/50th TFW at Hahn AB, Germany, on 30 January 1967. During its time with the wing it also completed a loan period with the 49th TFW. The 417th was reassigned to the 67th TRW (mainly an RF-4C wing) at Mountain Home AFB, Idaho, on 15 July 1968. The jet changed its codes to HE when it rejoined the 49th TFW on 15 November 1970. Following PDM in the spring of 1972, the F-4 was reassigned to the 13th TFS/432nd TRW on 22 June 1972. It then moved to the 18th TFW on 27 June 1975. After a further PDM at Ogden ALC in the winter of 1979-80, the fighter was reassigned to the 31st TFW/TTW from 11 April

1980 until its retirement on 21 April 1988. The aircraft is currently on display at the New England Air Museum in Windsor Locks, Connecticut.

27
F-4D-29-MC 66-7468 of Maj H L McKee and Capt J E Dubler, 555th TFS/432nd TRW, Udorn RTAB, 28 December 1972
This *Combat Tree* F-4D was delivered new to the 479th TFW on 28 January 1967. It was then transferred to the 8th TFW's 479th TFS (FP), via Ogden AMA, on 20 August 1968. It remained with the squadron until 10 August 1972, when the F-4 was reassigned to the 432nd TRW's 555th TFS. On 27 June 1975 the jet moved to the 18th TFW. It then served with the 31st TFW from 23 March 1980 until its retirement in October 1987. In March of the following year 66-7468 was put on display at Capitol Airport in Springfield, Illinois.

COLOUR SECTION

1
This LORAN-equipped F-4D carries a single AIM-4D missile among its ordnance. Despite its poor performance in *Rolling Thunder*, the missile was retained as the secondary armament for many F-4Ds during *Linebacker*, although it scored no MiG kills in 1972-73. The missile worked better when protected inside the missile bays of F-102 and F-106 interceptors, for its delicate sensors suffered weather attrition on the exposed F-4D pylons (*via Michael France*)

2
Early F-4Es with short gun barrels made their first appearance at Korat RTAFB on 17 November 1968, when 16 JV-coded aircraft flew in to replace the F-105s of the 469th TFS 'Fighting Bulls' as part of Operation *47 Buck 9*. Arriving in-theatre shortly after the end of *Rolling Thunder*, they had to wait until June 1972 to score their first MiG kill. The sharksmouths seen on these jets were a constant source of friction between the unit and higher authority, and they often vanished just prior to a base inspection taking place, only to reappear soon afterwards (*USAF via Col R Thurlow*)

3
By the time it had acquired the nickname *Bushwacker* on its nose-gear door, MiG killer F-4D 66-8734 had been modified with LORAN. It is seen here with Paveway LGBs (*via Peter Schinkelshoek*)

4
MiG killers (from left to right) Mike Vahue, Jim Null, Jeff Feinstein, Dan Cherry, Fred Olmsted and Stu Maas enjoy an NCO Club 'wetdown' after their three victories on 16 April 1972 (*Mike Vahue*)

5
MiG killer Leigh Hodgdon snapped this 'Wolfpack' F-4D trio on a mission in 1972. The nearest aircraft

(66-7750) was a MiG-killer for Maj W L Kirk and 1Lt T R Bongartz in October 1967. The jet came under 432nd TRW control in 1974 (*Leigh Hodgdon*)

6
Ex-35th TFS F-4D-29-MC 66-0232 was one of the precious few *Combat Tree* jets at Udorn in early 1972, where it is seen in January of that year with an AIM-4D Falcon and an ALQ-101 ECM pod on its left inboard pylon. Later recoded OC, the jet was used by the 13th TFS until it was downed by a SAM near Yen Bai during a CAP mission on 6 June 1972. Both pilot Maj James Fowler and WSO Capt John Seuell were killed (*via Michael J France*)

7
F-4E 67-0210 displays Maj P W Handley and 1Lt J J Smallwood's MiG kill as it rolls out with a load of CBU-24 for another mission North. 'Hands' Handley went on to command the 22nd TFS and then the 405th TFW, completing a 26-year USAF career. His WSO, and best friend, John Smallwood was less fortunate, for on 16 June 1973 his F-4E (67-0374) became the last US aircraft lost to enemy action during the conflict when it fell to ground fire in Cambodia. He and his pilot, Capt Sam Cornelius, were the last American airmen to die in that conflict (*Col Bill F McDonald*)

8
Lt Col Von Christiansen (469th TFS Ops Officer) and Maj Kaye Harden gave the 388th TFW its first MiG kill of the *Linebacker* period when they shot down a MiG-21 on 21 June 1972 in this aircraft, F-4E 67-0283. The aircraft features an original short-barrelled gun, which emitted a high-pitched shrieking noise when fired. It also failed to dissipate gun gas, which could then be ingested by the engine, causing power loss. By mid-1970 an improved, elongated Midas IV mount had been developed (*Don Logan*)

9
Thumbs up from Capts Mike Massen (WSO) and Fred Sheffler, 336th TFS MiG killers on 15 August 1972. Their unit had just completed an operational readiness inspection when it was deployed, with the 334th TFS, from Seymour Johnson AFB in response to the invasion of South Vietnam. As Fred Sheffler remembered it, 'Our wives were told only that we were going to South-east Asia. We deployed in two hops – the first all the way to Hawaii – but we didn't know our final destination. The guys on the C-141 support aircraft were told they were going to Udorn. When the C-141 ramp went down they saw it was actually Ubon. The destination had been changed mid-flight, and the folks at Ubon had no notice that our squadron was right behind the C-141!' (*Fred Sheffler*)

10
Takhli RTAFB KC-135 'boomer' John Huggins snapped this 4th TFS F-4E in 1972. It has the names of MiG killers Capts Sam White and Frank

Bettine on its yellow canopy rails, as well as a full load of AIM-9Es (*Steve Huggins via M France*)

11
Capts Steve Ritchie and Chuck DeBellevue pose with F-4D 66-7463, its five kills specially repainted with white backgrounds to show up in the press photos that were taken on 28-29 August 1972. Crew Chief Reggie Taylor (whose name appears on the crew panel) overpainted the jet's *Combat Tree* placard to fit all the stars on (*USAF*)

12
The 308th TFS managed to paint one of its aircraft with a sharksmouth (echoed in miniature on the wing-tanks) before, as maintenance chief Bill McDonald explained, 'the 432nd TRW and PACAF spoiled the party' as far as nose-art was concerned. This F-4E (67-0239) has a full air-to-air MiGCAP weapons fit (*Col Bill F McDonald*)

13
F-4E-32-MC 66-0313, from the second production batch of E-models, was a MiG killer for Capt C D Barton and 1Lt G D Watson, who shared a MiG-19 with Maj Clouser and 1Lt Brunson on 6 October 1972 (*JEM via Col R Thurlow*)

14
Bill McDonald with *THE WARLOCK*, which was one of his charges as 308th TFS maintenance chief. As a 'summer help' TDY squadron, his unit had to fight for equal access to base facilities with the permanent units (*Col Bill McDonald*)

15
Champagne for 'Chevy' flight after their 15 October MiG kill. These men are, standing, from left to right, Dave Coatsworth, Fred Brown, Ivy McCoy, Denver Rawlings (kneeling), Bobby Wayne and Rick Gibbs. Behind them is F-4D 66-7463, at rest after its sixth, and final, kill (*Ivy McCoy*)

16
F-4D 66-7463 at Udorn with its final MiG kill 'scoreboard' (*Col R Thurlow*)

17
John Dubler (left) and Harry McKee with their MiG-killer F-4D 66-7468. On the night of their victory, Harry did not get his usual 'combat nap'. 'Usually, after John finished his system checks and everything was set up to enter North Vietnam, I would let John fly the aircraft and I would turn off the intercom and take a 15- to 20-minute nap. If he needed me he could shake the stick, which got my attention instantly. We were quite surprised when *Combat Tree* detected an enemy contact coming our way out of North Vietnam. It was apparent that the bandit was moving fast, and climbing. I was established on an ingress heading of 010, and I held that all the way through the engagement, only clearing to the west to avoid the debris of the exploding MiG nine minutes later' (*Harry McKee*)

INDEX

References to illustrations are shown in **bold**. Plates are shown
with page and caption locators in brackets, with 'insignia' plates
having an 'I' prefix.

Accup, Sgt Steve **38**
Allen, Capt Ed 72, **72**
Autrey, 1Lt Dan L pl.**17**(55, 92), 64, **69**

Baily, Lt Col Carl 42, **47**
Baily, Lt Col Griff **72**
Barnes, Gene P **49**
Barton, Capt Charles D pl.**21**(56, 93), cs.**13**(61, 95), 67
Beatty, Capt James M **33**, 34–35, **34**, pl.**7**(52, 91)
Becker, Capt Al **72**
Beckers, Lt Col Lyle C 'Sky King' **33**, 34, 64, **65**
Bettine, Capt Frank E 46–47, pl.**14**(54, 92), cs.**10**(60, 95)
Boeing KC-135: **24**, **39**, cs.**5**(59, 94–95)
Bongartz, 1Lt T R cs.**5**(59, 94–95)
Brown, Maj Fred **4**, 10, pl.**23**(57, 93), cs.**15**(61, 95), 77–78
Brown, Lt Col J E pl.**26**(58, 94)
Brunson, 1Lt Cecil H pl.**20**(56, 93), 67, 70, **70**, 71, 93, 95
Brunson, Lt Col Jim **49**, **79**, 80, **80**, 81

Case, Capt Randy **75**
Cherry, Maj (later Brig Gen) E Dan 13, 18, **18**, 19–20, **19**, 21, 22,
    22, pl.**3**(50, 90), cs.**4**(59, 94)
Christiansen, Lt Col Von R 38–39, **39**, pl.**9**(52, 91), cs.**8**(60, 95)
Clouser, Maj Gordon L pl.**20**(56, 93), 67–69, 95
Coatsworth, Dave cs.**15**(61, 95)
Coe, Capt Richard E 'Dick' pl.**19**(56, 93), 66, 67
Cooney, Lt Col James P 'Jim' **31**, 32, 33, 46
Cooper, Col Mike 6, 10–11, 12, 13, 23, 26–28, 41, 71, 78–79
Cornelius, Capt Sam 95
Crane, Capt Greg **18**, 20, 21, 22
Crews, Maj Barton P **17**, 25–26, 30, **31**

DeBellevue, Capt Charles B 'Chuck' 10, **46**, 49, pl.**16**(55, 92),
    62, 63
    with Capt Ritchie **4**, 28, 29, 40, **40**, 41, 47, pl.**6**(51, 90–91),
    pl.**11**(53, 91), pl.**15**(54, 92), cs.**11**(60, 95)
Diehl, 1Lt William C pl.**24**(57, 93–94), 73, **74**
Dubler, Capt John pl.**27**(58, 94), cs.**17**(61, 95), 82, **82**, 83

Eaves, Capt Steve D **22**, 28, 29, **31**, pl.**5**(51, 90)
Erickson, Lt Col **13**
Ettel, Lt Cdr Mike, USN 43, **43**

Feinstein, Capt Jeff S **31**, 35, 36, 42, 47, **47**, **49**, 72, **72**, 73
    with Maj Cherry **18**, 22, pl.**3**(50, 90)
Ferguson, Lt Col **64**
Fowler, Maj James 95
Frye, Lt Col Wayne T 'Fossil' 32, 33, **46**

Gabriel, Col Charles A **31**
Gibbs, Rick cs.**15**(61, 95)
Gutman, Sgt Mike **21**

Handley, Maj Phil W 'Hands' **37**, 38, **38**, pl.**8**(52, 91), pl.**7**(60, 95)
Harden, Maj Kaye M 38–39, **39**, pl.**9**(52, 91), cs.**8**(60, 95)
Hardgrave, Capt Doug 46, **49**, **80**
Hardy, Capt Richard F 'Tuna' 39, 40, pl.**10**(53, 91)
Hargrove, 1Lt William S 'Bud' **43**, pl.**18**(55, 93), 63, **63**, 65, 73
Harris, Maj Jeff 29–30
Hendrickson, Capt James L pl.**25**(58, 94), 74–75, **75**, 76–77, **76**
Hildreth, Brig Gen 43
Hodgdon, 1Lt Leigh A **7**, 14–15, cs.**5**(59, 94–95)
Holtz, Maj R Lon pl.**24**(57, 93–94), 73–74, **74**
Hope, Bob **80**
Howman, Capt Paul 84–85
Hudson, Maj Sidney 32–33
Huggins, John cs.**10**(60, 95)
Huwe, Capt John **33**, 34

Imaye, Capt Stan M 40, 42, pl.**12**(53, 92), 85

Jasperson, Capt R H 'Bob' pl.**22**(57, 93), **64**, **65**, 69–70, **70**
Jeffcoat, Maj C H 92
Jones, Capt (later Lt Col) Keith W 'Bill' **17**, 25–26, 30, **31**, 72, **72**

Katz, Capt Milt **37**
Kay, Lt Col Bob 92
Kikta, Maj John **7**
Kiloran, Jim **48**
Kirk, Maj W L cs.**5**(59, 94–95)
Kittinger, Lt Col Joe W **7**, 14–15, **15**, 32
Kyle, Maj Bill **65**

Leonard, Capt Bruce 6, 8, 35–36, 41–42
Lewinski, Capt Paul T 39, 40, pl.**10**(53, 91)

Locher, 1Lt (later Capt) Roger C 14, **14**, 26, 28, 29, 30, 31–32, **38**,
    46, pl.**1**(50, 90)
Lodge, Maj Robert A 'Bob' 14, **14**, 17, 26, 27, 28, 29, 30–31, **36**,
    pl.**1**(50, 90)
Logeman, Capt Don **9**
Lorenz, Gary 23, **23**
Lucas, Maj Jon 47–49, **48**
Lueders, Maj Ernie **64**, **65**

Maas, Capt Stu 8–9, 13, 16, 17, 18–21, 22, 23, cs.**4**(59, 94)
Madden, Capt John 7, 31, 36–37, **36**, **40**, 47, **49**, 65, 71–72
    with Capt DeBellevue 10, 49, pl.**16**(55, 92), 62–64, **62**
Malloy, Capt Frank E 46–47, pl.**14**(54, 92), cs.**10**(60, 95)
Markle, 1Lt (later Lt Col) John D 6, **22**, 28, 29, 30–31, **31**, **46**,
    pl.**5**(51, 90)
Massak, Capt Mark A 43, 45, pl.**13**(54, 92), cs.**9**(60, 95)
McCoy, 1Lt Fred **9**
McCoy, Maj Ivy **4**, 10, pl.**23**(57, 93), cs.**15**(61, 95), 77–78
McDonald, Col Bill 10, 19, 21–22, 27, 31, **38**, cs.**12**(60, 95),
    cs.**14**(61, 95)
McDonnell Douglas F-4 Phantom II cs.**14**(61, 95), **73**
    ECM pods **34**, cs.**6**(60, 95), **62**, **78**
    fuel tanks, centreline **11**, 19
    IFF interrogation devices, *Combat Tree* 8, 15–16, 20, 28, 80
McDonnell Douglas F-4D 6–7, **6**, **24**, **44**, cs.**5**(59, 94–95), **65**, **74**,
    83
    F-4D-24-MC **9**
    F-4D-28-MC **12**
    F-4D-29-MC
        65-0784: 14, 16, pl.**1**(50, 90)
        66-0230: 15, 16, 16-17, **17**, pl.**2**(50, 90)
        66-0232 cs.**6**(60, 95)
        66-0267 pl.**16**(55, 92), **62**
        66-0269 pl.**26**(58, 94), 80
        66-0280 pl.**4**(51, 90)
        66-7463: 14, 15–16, 18, **22**, 26, 47, **48**, pl.**6**(51, 90–91),
            pl.**15**(54, 92), pl.**23**(57, 93), cs.**11**(60, 95), cs.**15**,
            16(61, 95), 77, **77**
        66-7468 pl.**27**(58, 94), cs.**17**(61, 95), 82, **82**
        66-7501: 72, **72**
    F-4D-31-MC **11**, **18**, pl.**3**(50, 90)
    F-4D-32-MC **22**, pl.**5**(51, 90), cs.**3**(59, 94)
    LORAN-equipped **24**, 30–31, cs.**1**(59, 94)
McDonnell Douglas F-4E 6, 7-8, **10**, 16, **21**, **34**, cs.**2**(59, 94),
    cs.**10**(60, 95), **74**, **78**
    67-0230: **73**
    67-0239: 43, cs.**12**(60, 95)
    67-0240: 66
    67-0281: **33**
    67-0354: **62**
    67-0385: **39**
    69-0276: 70, **70**, 71
    F-4E-32-MC pl.**21**(56, 93), cs.**13**(61, 95), 67, **67**
    F-4E-33-MC **38**, 40, pl.**8**(52, 91), cs.**7**(60, 95)
    F-4E-34-MC pl.**6**(51, 90–91), pl.**12**(53, 92), pl.**17**(55, 92),
        pl.**25**(58, 94), **69**, **75**, 76
    F-4E-35-MC
        67-0283: **39**, pl.**9**(52, 91), cs.**8**(60, 95)
        67-0301: **7**, pl.**24**(57, 93–94), **74**
        67-0309: 13
        67-0315: **39**, 41
        67-0333: **33**, **34**, pl.**7**(52, 91)
        67-0337: **37**, 81
    F-4E-36-MC 40, **40**, 48, pl.**11**(53, 91), pl.**20**(56, 93), 67
    F-4E-37-MC 38, cs.**18**(55, 93), 65
    F-4E-40-MC pl.**19**(56, 93)
    F-4E-42-MC 46, pl.**14**(54, 92), pl.**22**(57, 93)
    F-4E-43-MC 43, pl.**13**(54, 92)
    F-4E-45-MC 68, **75**
    gun mount, Midas IV **39**, cs.**8**(60, 95)
    Rivet Haste slatted wing **40**, 78
McDonnell Douglas RF-4C **74**
McKee, Maj Harry L pl.**27**(58, 94), cs.**17**(61, 95), 82–83, **82**, **84**
Mikoyan
    MiG-17: 12, 85
    MiG-19: 49, 69
    MiG-19S 'Farmer' (Shenyang J-6) 25
    MiG-21: **4**, 12, 85
Muldoon, 1Lt **44**
Murphy, Capt Terry **36**, 63

Newman, Maj Sam **36**
Nixon, President Richard 12, 13, 25, 73, 79
North American T-28: **74**
Null, Capt Jim C 23, **23**, **31**, pl.**4**(51, 90), cs.**4**(59, 94)

Ochandarena, Doug **80**
Olmsted Jr, Capt Frederick S 'Fredo' 15, **15**, 16–17, 18–19, **19**,
    20, 21, **22**, **31**, pl.**2**(50, 90), cs.**4**(59, 94)

Pettit, Capt Larry H 'Doc' 28, **31**, 32–33, 36, **46**, 71, 72
Pickett, Maj R Stan 16, pl.**26**(58, 94), **79**, 80–82, **80**

Rawlings, Denver cs.**15**(61, 95)

Retterbush, Maj Gary L pl.**17**(55, 92), pl.**22**(57, 93), 64, 69–70, **69**, **70**
Richard, Capt Larry, USMC 43, **43**
Ritchie, Capt R Steve 27, 31, **31**, 35, 36, **36**, 37, **46**, 77
    with Capt DeBellevue **4**, 28, 29, 40–41, **40**, 47, pl.**6**(51,
    90–91), pl.**11**(53, 91), pl.**15**(54, 92), cs.**11**(60, 95)
Rodriguez, Sgt **76**
Rubus, Capt Gary M pl.**25**(58, 94), 74, 75, **75**, 76, **76**, 77

Sam, Nguyen Tien 42, 64, 66
Sheffler, Capt Fred 43–45, **45**, pl.**13**(54, 92), cs.**9**(60, 95)
Smallwood, 1Lt John J 37, **38**, pl.**8**(52, 91), cs.**7**(60, 95)
Smith, Col Scott G **47**, 84
Soat, Nguyen Duc 70, **70**, 93
Squier, Lt Col **44**
Summers, Capt Bob **75**
Sumner, 1Lt James M **33**, 34, **34**, pl.**7**(52, 91)

Taft, Lt Col T E 'Gene' 42, pl.**12**(53, 92), 85
Taylor, Sgt Reginald **4**, 47, cs.**11**(60, 95), 92
Thurlow, Col Ron **13**, 79
Tibbett, Capt C Bryan 43, pl.**18**(55, 93), 62, 63, **63**, 65, 73
Trimble, 1Lt J R 92

Udorn RTAFB **27**

United States Air Force
    squadrons
        4th TFS **33**, **34**, **40**, 42, 46, **46**, pl.**10**(53, 91), pl.**12**(53, 92),
            pl.**14**(54, 92), cs.**10**(60, 95)
        13th TFS 'Black Panthers' 16–17, **17**, **18**, 28, 42, pl.**2**,
            3(50, 90), pl.**26**(58, 94), cs.**6**(60, 95), 72
        14th TRS **74**
        24th TFS **21**
        25th TFS **24**, 41
        34th TFS **10**, **39**, **41**, 47–48, pl.**19**, **21**, **22**, **24**(56–57,
            93–94), 66–67, **67**, 73, **73**, **74**
        35th TFS 'Rams' 33–34, **34**, **48**, pl.**7**(52, 91), **64**, **65**,
            67–69, 78
        58th TFS 13, 37–38, **40**, 43, pl.**8**(52, 91), pl.**11**(53, 91), 78,
            78
        307th TFS pl.**25**(58, 94), 63, **66**, **68**, 75, **76**, 78
        308th TFS 13, 37, **37**, cs.**12**(60, 95), cs.**14**(61, 95), **62**, **74**,
            75, **76**, **77**, 81
        309th TFS 48
        336th TFS 'Rocketeers' 43–45, pl.**13**(54, 92), 95
        390th TFS 'Wild Boars' **6**, 11
        421st TFS **33**
        435th TFS **9**, 41, **44**
        469th TFS **13**, **39**, pl.**9**(52, 91), pl.**17**(55, 92), pl.**20**(56, 93),
            69, 78
        523rd TFS **22**, 23, **23**, 24, pl.**4**(51, 90), 78
        555th TFS 'Triple Nickel' 10, **12**, **13**, 14–15, **24**, 28, 32,
            41, **46**, pl.**1**(50, 90), pl.**5**, **6**(51, 90–91), cs.**15**,
            16(54–55, 92), pl.**18**(55, 93), pl.**23**(57, 93), pl.**27**(58,
            94), 65, **74**, 79–80, **79**, 81–83
    wings
        4th TFW 38, 64, 79
        8th TFW 13, **24**, 27, 43
        31st TFW 75, **76**, 79
        366th TFW **34**, 39, 46
        388th TFW 39, cs.**8**(60, 95), 64, 73
        432nd TRW 10, 13, 16, 17, 27, 30, **31**, **34**, 37, 42, **49**, 74,
            74, **77**, **84**

Vahue, Capt Mike D 23, **23**, 24, pl.**4**(51, 90), cs.**4**(59, 94)
Vietnamese Peoples' Air Force (VPAF) 12, 25, 29, 32, 33, 37, 39,
    42, 49
Vogt Jr, Gen John W 31, **31**
Volloy, Capt Gerald R 15, 16–17, pl.**2**(50, 90)

Watson, 1Lt George D pl.**21**(56, 93), cs.**13**(61, 95), 67
Wayne, Col Robert 'Bobby' cs.**15**(61, 95), 77, 78
weapons
    bombs, CBU-24 cs.**7**(60, 95), **68**, **75**
    bombs, Mk 82: **10**, **20**, **34**, 81
    bombs, Paveway laser-guided (LGB) **9**, cs.**3**(59, 94), 66
    cannon, M61A-1: **34**, cs.**8**(60, 95)
    missiles
        AIM-4D Falcon 10–11, 24, cs.**1**(59, 94), cs.**6**(60, 95)
        AIM-7 Sparrow 7, 10, 11, **39**, **78**
        AIM-7E-2 'Dogfight' 10, 11, **20**, **22**, **30**, **62**
        AIM-9 Sidewinder 7, 11, 21-22
        AIM-9E **9**, 10, **21**, **22**, 37, **62**
        AIM-9J 9-10, **35**, **62**, 63-64, **78**
Webb III, 1Lt Ken 66, 67
Webb, 1Lt O E pl.**19**(56, 93)
Wells, TSgt **76**
Westphal, Lt Col Curtis 72–73, **72**, 83
White, Capt Sam E 46–47, pl.**14**(54, 92), cs.**10**(60, 95)
Wilkinson, Capt Dennis 29-30
Williams, 1Lt **13**

Young, 1Lt Bill **21**
Young, Capt Joe 93
Young, Capt Myron **70**, 71